15 Days of Prayer
With Meister Eckhart

Also in the *15 Days of Prayer* collection:

15 DAYS OF PRAYER
WITH
Meister Eckhart

ANDRÉ GOZIER, O.S.B.

Translated by Victoria Hébert and Denis Sabourin

Liguori
LIGUORI, MISSOURI

Published by Liguori Publications
Liguori, Missouri
http://www.liguori.org

This book is a translation of *Prier 15 Jours Avec Maître Eckhart (ou la naissance de Dieu en l'âme)*, published by Nouvelle Cité, 1992, Montrouge, France.

Library of Congress Cataloging-in-Publication Data

Gozier, André.
    [Prier 15 Jours avec Maître Eckhart. English]
    15 days of prayer with Meister Eckhart / André Gozier ; Victoria Hébert and Denis Sabourin, translators. — 1st English ed.
        p. cm.
    Includes bibliographical references.
    ISBN 0-7648-0652-1
    1. Eckhart, Meister, d. 1327—Meditations. 2. Spiritual life—Catholic Church. I. Title: Fifteen days of prayer with Meister Eckhart. II. Title.

BV5095.E3 G6413 2000
269'.6—dc21   00–056947

Scripture quotations are taken from the *New Revised Standard Version Bible*, copyright 1989 by the Division of Christian Education of the National Council of the Churches of Christ in the U.S.A. Used by permission. All rights reserved.

Printed in the United States of America
04 03 02 01 00   5 4 3 2 1
First English Edition 2000

Table of Contents

How to Use This Book

AN OLD CHINESE PROVERB, or at least what I am able to recall of what is supposed to be an old Chinese proverb, goes something like this: "Even a journey of a thousand miles begins with a single step." When you think about it, the truth of the proverb is obvious. It is impossible to begin any project, let alone a journey, without taking the first step. I think it might also be true, although I cannot recall if another Chinese proverb says it, "that the first step is often the hardest." Or, as someone else once observed, "the distance between a thought and the corresponding action needed to implement the idea takes the most energy." I don't know who shared that perception with me but I am certain it was not an old Chinese master!

With this ancient proverbial wisdom, and the not-so-ancient wisdom of an unknown contemporary sage still fresh, we move from proverbs to presumptions. How do these relate to the task before us?

I am presuming that if you are reading this introduction it is because you are contemplating a journey. My presumption is that you are preparing for a spiritual journey and that you have taken at least some of the first steps necessary to prepare for this journey. I also presume, and please excuse me if I am making too many presumptions, that in your preparation for the spiritual journey you have determined that you need a guide.

From deep within the recesses of your deepest self, there was something that called you to consider Meister Eckhart as a potential companion. If my presumptions are correct, may I congratulate you on this decision? I think you have made a wise choice, a choice that can be confirmed by yet another source of wisdom, the wisdom that comes from practical experience.

Even an informal poll of experienced travelers will reveal a common opinion; it is very difficult to travel alone. Some might observe that it is even foolish. Still others may be even stronger in their opinion and go so far as to insist that it is necessary to have a guide, especially when you are traveling into uncharted waters and into territory that you have not yet experienced. I am of the personal opinion that a traveling companion is welcome under all circumstances. The thought of traveling alone, to some exciting destination without someone to share the journey with does not capture my imagination or channel my enthusiasm. However, with that being noted, what is simply a matter of preference on the normal journey becomes a matter of necessity when a person embarks on a spiritual journey.

The spiritual journey, which can be the most challenging of all journeys, is experienced best with a guide, a companion, or at the very least, a friend in whom you have placed your trust. This observation is not a preference or an opinion but rather an established spiritual necessity. All of the great saints with whom I am familiar had a spiritual director or a confessor who journeyed with them. Admittedly, at times the saint might well have traveled far beyond the experience of their guide and companion but more often than not they would return to their director and reflect on their experience. Understood in this sense, the director and companion provided a valuable contribution and necessary resource.

When I was learning how to pray (a necessity for anyone who desires to be a full-time and public "religious person"), the community of men that I belong to gave me a great gift. Between my second and third year in college, I was given a one-year sabbatical, with all expenses paid and all of my personal needs met. This period of time was called novitiate. I was officially designated as a novice, a beginner in the spiritual journey, and I was assigned a "master," a person who was willing to lead me. In addition to the master, I was provided with every imaginable book and any other resource that I could possibly need. Even with all that I was provided, I did not learn how to pray because of the books and the unlimited resources, rather it was the master, the companion who was the key to the experience.

One day, after about three months of reading, of quiet and solitude, and of practicing all of the methods and descriptions of prayer that were available to me, the master called. "Put away the books, forget the method, and just listen." We went into a room, became quiet, and tried to recall the presence of God, and then, the master simply prayed out loud and permitted me to listen to his prayer. As he prayed, he revealed his hopes, his dreams, his struggles, his successes, and most of all, his relationship with God. I discovered as I listened that his prayer was deeply intimate but most of all it was self-revealing. As I learned about him, I was led through his life experience to the place where God dwells. At that moment I was able to understand a little bit about what I was supposed to do if I really wanted to pray.

The dynamic of what happened when the master called, invited me to listen, and then revealed his innermost self to me as he communicated with God in prayer, was important. It wasn't so much that the master was trying to reveal to me what needed to be said; he was not inviting me to pray with the same words that he used, but rather that he was trying to bring me to that place within myself where prayer becomes possible. That place, a place of intimacy and of self-awareness, was a necessary stop on the journey and it was a place that I needed to be led to. I could not have easily discovered it on my own.

The purpose of the volume that you hold in your hand is to lead you, over a period of fifteen days or, maybe more realistically, fifteen prayer periods, to a place where prayer is possible. If you already have a regular experience and practice of prayer, perhaps this volume can help lead you to a deeper place, a more intimate relationship with the Lord.

It is important to note that the purpose of this book is not to lead you to a better relationship with Meister Eckhart, your spiritual companion. Although your companion will invite you to share some of their deepest and most intimate thoughts, your companion is doing so only to bring you to that place where God dwells. After all, the true measurement of a companion for the journey is that they bring you to the place where you need to be, and then they step back, out of the picture. A guide who brings you to the desired destination and then sticks around is a very unwelcome guest!

Many times I have found myself attracted to a particular idea or method for accomplishing a task, only to discover that what seemed to be inviting and helpful possessed too many details. All of my energy went to the mastery of the details and I soon lost my enthusiasm. In each instance, the book that seemed so promising ended up on my bookshelf, gathering dust. I can assure you, it is not our intention that this book end up in your bookcase, filled with promise, but unable to deliver.

There are three simple rules that need to be followed in order to use this book with a measure of satisfaction.

Place: It is important that you choose a place for reading that provides the necessary atmosphere for reflection and that does not allow for too many distractions. Whatever place you choose needs to be comfortable, have the necessary lighting, and, finally, have a sense of "welcoming" about it. You need to be able to look forward to the experience of the journey. Don't travel steerage if you know you will be more comfortable in first class and if the choice is realistic for you. On the other hand, if first class is a distraction and you feel more comfortable and more yourself in steerage, then it is in steerage that you belong.

My favorite place is an overstuffed and comfortable chair in my bedroom. There is a light over my shoulder, and the chair reclines if I feel a need to recline. Once in a while, I get lucky and the sun comes through my window and bathes the entire room in light. I have other options and other places that are available to me but this is the place that I prefer.

Time: Choose a time during the day when you are most alert and when you are most receptive to reflection, meditation, and prayer. The time that you choose is an essential component. If you are a morning person, for example, you should choose a time that is in the morning. If you are more alert in the afternoon, choose an afternoon time slot; and if evening is your preference, then by all means choose the evening. Try to avoid "peak" periods in your daily routine when you know that you might be disturbed. The time that you choose needs to be your time and needs to work for you.

It is also important that you choose how much time you

will spend with your companion each day. For some it will be possible to set aside enough time in order to read and reflect on all the material that is offered for a given day. For others, it might not be possible to devote one time to the suggested material for the day, so the prayer period may need to be extended for two, three, or even more sessions. It is not important how long it takes you; it is only important that it works for you and that you remain committed to that which is possible.

For myself I have found that fifteen minutes in the early morning, while I am still in my robe and pajamas and before my morning coffee, and even before I prepare myself for the day, is the best time. No one expects to see me or to interact with me because I have not yet "announced" the fact that I am awake or even on the move. However, once someone hears me in the bathroom, then my window of opportunity is gone. It is therefore important to me that I use the time that I have identified when it is available to me.

Freedom: It may seem strange to suggest that freedom is the third necessary ingredient, but I have discovered that it is most important. By freedom I understand a certain "stance toward life," a "permission to be myself and to be gentle and understanding of who I am." I am constantly amazed at how the human person so easily sets himself or herself up for disappointment and perceived failure. We so easily make judgments about ourselves and our actions and our choices, and very often those judgments are negative, and not at all helpful.

For instance, what does it really matter if I have chosen a place and a time, and I have missed both the place and the time for three days in a row? What does it matter if I have chosen, in that twilight time before I am completely awake and still a little sleepy, to roll over and to sleep for fifteen minutes more? Does it mean that I am not serious about the journey, that I really don't want to pray, that I am just fooling myself when I say that my prayer time is important to me? Perhaps, but I prefer to believe that it simply means that I am tired and I just wanted a little more sleep. It doesn't mean anything more than that. However, if I make it mean more than that, then I can become discouraged, frustrated, and put myself into a state where I might more easily give up. "What's the use? I might as well forget all about it."

The same sense of freedom applies to the reading and the praying of this text. If I do not find the introduction to each day helpful, I don't need to read it. If I find the questions for reflection at the end of the appointed day repetitive, then I should choose to close the book and go my own way. Even if I discover that the reflection offered for the day is not the one that I prefer and that the one for the next day seems more inviting, then by all means, go on to the one for the next day.

That's it! If you apply these simple rules to your journey you should receive the maximum benefit and you will soon find yourself at your destination. But be prepared to be surprised. If you have never been on a spiritual journey you should know that the "travel brochures" and the other descriptions that you might have heard are nothing compared to the real thing. There is so much more than you can imagine.

A final prayer of blessing suggests itself:

> Lord, catch me off guard today.
> Surprise me with some moment of beauty
>   or pain
> So that at least for the moment
> I may be startled into seeing that you are
>   here in all your splendor,
> Always and everywhere,
> Barely hidden,
> Beneath,
> Beyond,
> Within this life I breathe.
>
> —*Frederick Buechner*

REV. THOMAS M. SANTA, CSsR
LIGUORI, MISSOURI
FEAST OF THE PRESENTATION, 1999

A Brief Chronology
of Meister Eckhart's Life

THE SEARCH FOR GOD and the experience of God has neither nationality nor age; it is a process where man is being lifted towards a transcendence which goes beyond all human contingencies.

Eckhart, famous yet unknown. Famous, because of his trial with the ecclesiastical authorities. Unknown, because of the "deepness" of his thinking. We admire him for his light and his boldness. We fear him because of his obscurity and requirements. Through his bold affirmations, he overturns our idols. Through his flashes, he awakens our sleeping consciences. Through his jostlings, he shakes our laziness. It is with this in mind that he hurls astounding formulae at his readers. To accept them "to the letter" would be to betray him. But under the ardor of his words, life is born in us again. He draws us towards fascinating peaks. He makes us look into dizzying chasms.

Eckhart: he is the air at the summits, a great wind of spiritual freedom, a stiff drink, oxygen that is able to renew a life of prayer that has become too cramped and stiff. He speaks of great problems, those upon which a spiritual life can be built: the Trinity, the divine being, creation, the relationship between what is created and what is not, the renunciation that is necessary for our union with the divine.

Eckhart's thoughts are dynamic. They bring up as many questions as they give explanations, they do not define themselves.

HIS LIFE

Who was Meister Eckhart? What do we know about this great spiritualist? In actual fact, we know very little.

c. 1260–1294:

Johannes Eckhart is presumed to have been born around the year 1260 in Hochheim (Germany); it is thought that he came from a well-to-do family.

c. 1275, he entered the Dominican Order at Erfurt and became a student (c. 1280) at their house in Cologne, which had been founded by Albert the Great.

c. 1294, he went to Paris to continue his studies where he found himself plunged into an intellectual milieu that was the liveliest in all of Christianity.

1298–1323:

Sometime before 1298, he was named prior at Erfurt and Vicar General of Thuringia.

c. 1302, he was sent to Paris a second time to study and teach as a "Master of sacred theology."

In 1303, he returned to Erfurt and was made provincial for Saxony (which, at that time, stretched from Holland to Livonia).

In 1307, he was appointed Vicar General for Bohemia.

1311 saw him again in Paris; later, in Strasbourg in 1314, he exercised some important duties and occupied numerous contemplative monasteries of the Rhine regions (until 1323).

1325–1329:

c. 1325, after a brilliant career, the ecclesiastical authorities in Cologne began to question him. Charges of heresy were uttered against him because of his sermons.

On February 13, 1327, Eckhart solemnly protested his orthodoxy and publicly stated that if there was anything wrong in his writings, he retracted it. This appears to be the last date where we have any information about Eckhart—it is believed that he died within days of his proclamation. He did not live to see his trial for heresy.

The archbishop of Cologne (Hermann von Virneburg) was very opposed to all of his works. He made no secret of his hatred for Eckhart and took his cause all the way to Avignon where Pope John XXII would later issue a Papal Bull (*In agro dominico*—at a later date—on March 27, 1329) in which a series of Eckhart's statements were, posthumously, characterized as heretical and others suspected of heresy.

For hundreds of years, knowledge of Eckhart and his writings was limited to a few pages in a few select history texts and in sermons by Johannes Tauler and Henry Suso until interest was revived in the late nineteenth century when two of his manuscripts were discovered.

No matter what one may think of Eckhart's philosophies and dogma, his ethical view was one of purity and sublimity. Man's "interiority" was his main concern. He spoke very little of Church ceremonies. Exterior penance had little value to him—he believed that man should turn himself directly to God and allow himself to be led by God's directions. God gives each person his/her special job and provides a means for that person to accomplish it. A flight from one's self, one's own will, and selflessness is the key to life. He is also very controversial because of his placement of Martha in a higher position than Mary—as she was at a higher stage of spiritual development.

Since 1980, steps have been taken by the Dominican Order to seek an official declaration from the pope to acknowledge "the exemplary character of Eckhart's activity and preaching and to recommend his writings (particularly the spiritual works, treatises, and sermons) as an expression of authentic Christian mysticism and as trustworthy guides to Christian life according to the spirit of the Gospel." (The Eckhart Society)

Introduction

THE CENTRAL THEME: Eckhart centered his message on what was essential: God comes to dwell within us as an incredible consequence of the Good News, "and the Word became flesh" (Jn 1:14). The grace of the Incarnation was in view of the grace of the indwelling of divine people.

> Why did God become man? So that God would be born into the soul and the soul would be born in God (JAH, Sermon 38).

It is then not the prerogative of a few privileged people. It must not seem to be impossible for one to have the Son born within him.

We will, then, spend fifteen days together by following the principle themes of Eckhart's spirituality: the axis being the birth of God in the soul.

Eckhart is the principle representative of this spiritual current that is called speculative mysticism, the mysticism of the being, or abstract mysticism, which is in contrast to a marital mysticism that is displayed mainly by Teresa of Ávila (1515–1582) or John of the Cross (1542–1591).

We will, from our perspective, call it the mysticism of the Exodus, that is, of the flight from Egypt, from multiplicity, in order to penetrate into the promised land of unity, for, with him, an ontological identity is not at work, but a peregrinate (traveling) identity, that is, that I can never say "I am" like God could say it.

Connected to this school of spirituality are the Beguin, Hadewijch of Anvers (thirteenth century), two great Dominicans: Johannes Tauler (c. 1300–1361) and Henry Suso (1295–1366), and a regular canon, Jan Van Ruysbroeck (1293–1381). The sources for this are mainly Augustine, Denys, Albert the Great, and neo-Platonism.

Hadewijch arranged some of Eckhart's themes, Tauler and Suso were disciples of the Master of Cologne, but they added little. Ruysbroeck, even though he distanced himself with respect to him, doubtlessly through prudence, owes him a great deal.

Eckhart wants to orient the souls who want to follow his teachings to an attitude of the soul that we will call "interiority." Through that, we mean the movement by which the spirit deepens itself in the search for its foundation.

For the moment, let us seek the introversion (contemplation) of our heart, that will be the way to deepen or elevate it (the same thing) until it unites with our principle, "interior intimo meo" (deeper than the very depth of my inner self), according to Saint Augustine.

Through that, we will also touch the methods of those who meditate (in Hinduism)—who are counseled to constantly ask themselves the question: who am I? At the beginning of this prayerful gathering—above all for those who do not claim Christ to be their Lord but who are drawn by Eckhart—we can again take up this questioning that is close to Ramana Maharshi's heart. Eckhart could be an invitation, for those people who look at things from an Eastern perspective, to deepen their Christianity. Here, they will find what they sought there...and much more.

Interiority, then, is the relationship between the individual and himself before the Absolute. It presupposes a descent into our inner selves, it necessitates that we withstand God's glance upon us and on our lives. We know that it will, at times, take on the form of a battle, of an intermittent future, marked by qualitative leaps and peaks. But man must build himself, he makes himself what he is. Interiority is one of the vital characteristics of a personality.

When man is too concerned with social relationships, or oriented towards a result that is too immediate, by living in the superficial zones of his being, he is often left well short of his inner being. The soul that remains on the surface of itself, that does not dwell within itself, is a stranger to itself. Eckhart makes this comparison: the man who doesn't have the habit of living within himself is like the man who, having wine in his cellar, doesn't know whether it is good unless he has tasted it.

Interiority makes us truly discover ourselves, God, and others. It is, therefore, very valuable. That is why, in order to discover our inner self, we must go beyond our "self." Do we know how to use it in order to truly "realize" our being?

For Eckhart, that would mean we must travel towards our very depth in order to realize the infinite wealth there. Interiority is like the field mentioned in the Gospel. Christ told us that there is a treasure in the depths of our soul; then, if we believe in his word—but do we truly believe in it?—we must take up shovels and picks to dig in the soil and discover the hidden treasure. Quickly, as soon as we have given it a few blows with the pick, the Lord, in his goodness, will let us find, not the hidden treasure (that would be too simple), but just a few gold nuggets, showing us that it is truly through interiority that we must seek the treasure (him). In brief, it is the discovery that the birth of God is realized in another dimension.

Also, when we want to be fraternal with those who go on a retreat with Eckhart, we have just a few words to say:

Search within
and you will find everything.

THE DIRECTIONS: After having indicated the axis of this retreat with Eckhart: the birth of God in the soul, we must have directions for the journey that is proposed.

Let us note that history, the Church, Mary, and man are not the things on which Eckhart particularly insists. What he was concerned with was the reality of God in the soul.

Above all, we will reflect with Eckhart upon the conditions for the search for God within ourselves. That will be the "Auditorium of the Spirit," for there are conditions. In Saint John's Gospel, Christ himself said: "Those who love me will keep my word, and my Father will love them, and we will come to them and make our home with them" (14:23).

What a wonderful thing! But there is an irrevocable condition: "Those who love me will keep my word."

Why are we not conscious of this divine presence within us? Eckhart replies: "Because you are not truly within your inner self": in your depth (M. Henry, *The Essence of the Manifestation*, vol. 2, PUF, 1963, p. 548).

God is in us, but we are not.

The directions for this journey will aim at helping you in this search.

After "The Auditorium of the Spirit" (Day One), we propose a meditation on themes that Eckhart held dear. First, "The Light" (Day Two), then the major axis: the "Birth" of God in the Soul (Day Three), but this is only possible with a certain "Detachment" (Day Four) by going all the way "Without Asking Why" (Day Five). It is that which will make us reach "The Depth of the Soul" (Day Six) and "The Search for the Model" (Day Seven). We also will insist on the theme "The Image" (Day Eight). All spiritual life comes up against "Suffering" (Day Nine)—we will see what Eckhart brings to us about this subject. All spiritual life comes up against action. We will see why Eckhart strangely chooses Martha and not Mary (Day Ten) and it will appear even more concrete than we could imagine. Then we will conclude with some of Eckhart's greatest themes which touch the summits of the spiritual life, for "Those Who Eat of Me Will Have a Greater Hunger" (Day Eleven). "The Desert" (Day Twelve), "The Opening" (Day Thirteen), and "Let God Reign in the Soul" (Day Fourteen) will give us a glimpse of Eckhart's boldness. The fifteenth and final day seeks to provoke an "awakening" of the depths of man, an awakening in man, and awakening of man in God.

Each chapter/day has at least two sub-sections in order to center our prayerful reflections, but the soul may freely pray through each passage that draws its attention.

The themes that are treated are presented like a spiral. We refer back to them at different levels of their depths (or heights—as they are one and the same thing). Eckhart is a difficult author; he is perhaps the greatest as well, in our opinion, along with Saint John of the Cross. Also, if we do not understand one of his passages, we must not be discouraged! We will come back to it later and it will seem more accessible to us then. The gaze of the person who prays with us will broaden itself. Eckhart will make him discover and penetrate into the deepest aspects of the mystery of interiority that he had not noticed before. Wasn't it the Holy Spirit's mission to lead the soul to interiority?

At the end of this fifteen-day retreat, we will have just scratched the surface of Eckhart's thinking. It is very rich, bold, and little is known about it. We have tried to avoid a few of his formulae which seem too excessive.

If this has helped us to pray, discover our interiority, and cultivate it, then we can thank him and perhaps consult the Bibliography (at the end of this book) to gain further insight or to better understand the paths which have been opened to us during our short time together with him.

We would also like to note that this book is neither a study of Meister Eckhart, nor an initiation to him, nor an anthology of him. This is not a book for reading—it is one for *meditation*. One must "pray with" Meister Eckhart, and undertake a prayerful reflection on his major themes. It is not for us to realize or understand all that he said—that would be impossible—but for it to give a spark to the soul, to help it have a certain spiritual energy by making it look towards the summits he describes. We must let ourselves be fascinated by the call of the mountain, be marveled through contact with it by the bounty of the wealth of its graces. Also, we must forgive him for certain missteps we might encounter here, those which we know to avoid according to the Papal Bull of John XXII.

Eckhart invites us to an adventure of the spirit which has its source in the Ultimate: he urges us to find our place (the depth of our soul and the depth of God) and to never stop ourselves at that which has already been gained.

Abbreviations
Used in This Book

AM   Sermons

D   About detachment, in the volume entitled "Tractates"

HN   About the noble man, in "Tractates"

IS   Spiritual instructions, in "Tractates"

JAH   German sermons, from translations by J. Ancelet-Hustache (Seuil Editions)

LCD   The Book of Divine Consolation, in "Tractates"

MSH   Sermons, from the translations by A. M. St. Hubert (Cahier du Sud Editions)

PP   Sermons, from the translation by P. Petit, NRF Editions

15 Days of Prayer
With Meister Eckhart

DAY ONE

The Auditorium of the Spirit

FOCUS POINT

Meister Eckhart stresses the immanence of God over God's transcendence as it concerns our experience of the Divine. That "God is within" is the reality that should draw our eyes to the Lord, so that we might gaze upon God present in our interior. So that we might see God within ourselves, we should seek solitude, and seek God in quiet and without distractions. All of our worries and concerns and distractions that might prevent us from seeing God within ourselves must be put behind us when we encounter God in this way, so that we might focus on him alone.

People often say to me: pray for me! Then I think: why do you look outside (of yourself)? Why don't you remain within your-

selves and draw from your own sense of goodness? You carry all truth essentially within yourself (JAH, Sermon 5b, "In hoc apparuit caritas Dei," p. 79).

———

Eckhart wants to lead us to the inner part of ourselves. With us, he wants to develop what Saint Paul called "the inner person." In order to hear God, we must be within our interior self, at home. This is how we commit ourselves to the path towards unity, which was so dear to the man from Thuringia, since, for him, whoever lives within their interior self is at home, and once there, that person tends to the unification of their being. Unity means solitude, solitude means a desert: these are some of the words that we see so often in Eckhart's works.

PUT ASIDE ALL OF YOUR WORRIES

Have no worries any longer; the Lord is close and he cares. So that the soul delights in the Lord, it must put aside all its worries, or at least at the time it gives itself to God. That is why Saint Paul said: put aside all of your worries, (for) the Lord is close and he cares, that is, he is in the most intimate part of ourselves when he finds us within ourselves and when the soul has not left to banter with the five senses (smell, touch, taste, hearing, and sight). The soul must be within itself, in the most intimate, elevated, and purest parts of its being and, furthermore, remain there at all times without looking to what is outside: that is where God is close and cares for us (JAH, Sermon 34, "Gaudete in Domino," p. 24).

What is necessary is a certainty that is given to us through faith and not felt as a presence. That could happen, but for the moment, what is essential is a feeling of God's presence through a "releasing of the reins" of our life. To know that God is caring and close to us will communicate to us a joyous conviction that will help us throughout this Eckhartian journey.

This presence is not located in the soul's powers (intelligence, memory, will), but within its center. That is why we don't perceive it.

We not only leave our worries and cares to God, but also our selves.

The self that must be left is not the true self, the one in which we will try to enter. The former operates in three zones: corporeity (the quality of being or having a material body), multiplicity, and temporality. The second only reveals itself little by little when we have reached a certain dimension of depth.

COUNT ON GOD

In another chapter, we will see another condition so that we will be able to listen to the Holy Spirit: detachment. But right now, it is enough to concentrate our effort on these two conditions to reach the birth of God in the soul:

- leave all worries aside
- abandonment of one's self

Why? Because, like our supporting text for today tells us: God is close, within the most intimate parts of ourselves. That is where we must search for him. We will adhere to the presence of God *within ourselves*. As it is said in Acts (17:28): "In him, we live and move and have our being," he envelops us from everywhere. With Saint Augustine we tell him: "Shelter me, Lord, and I will have been sheltered." Then, we will be able to hear what the Holy Spirit suggests to our deepest selves, for the kingdom of God [God himself] is "among you" (Lk 17:21). On this first day of our retreat, let us ask that our heart become an auditorium.

> When the Word speaks in the soul and the soul replies in the living Word, the Son comes to life in the soul (JAH, Sermon 18, "Adolescens, tibi dico," p. 163).

For:

> God is always close, but we aren't at all. God is close to us, but we are far from him. God is within, we are outside. God in us is at home, we are the strangers (PP, Sermon, "The kingdom of God is close," p. 94).

Don't be alarmed by what he could possibly ask of us:

> If God requires a great deal from man, that does not come from his severity, but from his great goodness: because what he wants is for the soul to grow so that it could receive a great deal and he has a great deal to give to it (PP, Sermon, "The kingdom of God is close," p. 94).

We must learn to rely upon God, to lean on him so that we can realize what he is to us:

> The birth of God in the soul: it must not seem impossible for anyone to reach that point. As difficult as that

could appear, what is it to me, since it is God—isn't it—who does it? All of his commandments are easy to obey!

I do not worry about what he commands me to do, what he wants, all of that is a small thing for me, as long as he gives me the grace to do it. Some people tell me that they don't have it! I reply: that makes me sad! But if you don't yearn for it, that makes me even sadder. If you can't have it, then have the desire to have it. If someone can no longer have this desire, they could have the desire to have this desire.... Let us be able to yearn like this for God, in such a way so that he has the desire, himself, to be born in us (PP, Sermon, "About Fulfillment," p. 18).

REFLECTION QUESTIONS

What are those worries and concerns in my life that prevent me from seeing God in my interior? What distractions and needless anxieties keep me from clearing an open space for God and experiencing him in my self? What techniques might I use to sharpen my focus on God's presence within me? Might I consider centering prayer or relaxation exercises as a possible aid in this endeavor?

DAY TWO

The Light

FOCUS POINT

When Jesus Christ was born into the world as flesh and blood, so too was he born into our hearts. And as he is the light of the world externally, so is his light the internal beacon that leads us to the Father. For what good is it for us to simply hear the Word and not internalize it? If that is the case—if we only hear it without acting upon it—then we are lost, we are not transformed, and we do not know God to the depths to which we are called.

My biological father is not totally my father, but only through a small bit of his nature and I am separate from him; he could be dead and I would still be alive. That is why the heavenly Father is truly my father, for I am his son and I have received everything that I have from him (JAH, Sermon 6, "Justi vivent in aeternum," p. 85).

T he light came to the world, it must enter into our hearts. The light is the Son who teaches us that we have a Father, that God is like a father for each of his children. But the Lord came amongst his people to make them become a multitude of brothers and his people did not receive him well. However, it is the light which enlightens all mankind who came into this world. We open our hearts to him, for we are destined to the very deepest intimate relationship with God.

INTERIORITY

In order to more easily enter into this divine intimate relationship, which will become interiority, we must explain it, for Eckhart's greatness lies in his keen sense of what interiority is.

All of the man-God's activities, which seem to be restricted to a particular locality and time—in Palestine—really happened everywhere. A "local" Christ is necessarily exterior, he is a model that is presented to us. A Christ that is seized through faith is, to the contrary, interior and, hence, universal. All of Jesus' actions are, in reality, actions that the Word fulfilled in consciences. What he did in the world of exteriority is just the trace of an action that is more secret, more real at the depth of hearts. Faith takes the exterior action and remakes it in man. The Gospel is called to be decoded at the very depth of the beings of the believers. The exterior action is the sign that refers back to an interior action. For example, the calmed storm is the sign by which the Lord calms all interior storms, all trials which upset the field of conscience, making a placid lake in which God can be reflected. Similarly, far from stalling us in a past world, the miracles in the Gospel lead us into an invisible world, that is, into the interior world, which each soul has within itself; a place where it touches eternity. That is why we should study certain symbols, especially in the Gospel of Saint John: light for the born-blind, water for the Samaritan, and so on. It is thus that Christ truly appears to the soul, like "the exegete of the Father." In the same way as Mary Magdalene touched his body with her hand [= material and limited contact], Thomas was invited to touch with the soul, to penetrate into the interiority of them in order to touch the risen Christ in them, for only faith truly touches.

Then we discover the truth of Saint Augustine's formula: "You were more interior to myself than I was," that is, more interior to my most intimate and most elevated [= deepest] depth. The spirit discovers God present in it, like it is beyond itself. "I sought you outside and you were inside," the Bishop of Hippo said. And finally, "There is someone greater than you within you." These are key phrases about interiority. Let us stop here in order to meditate on them.

We must reread the Gospel from this perspective. The stories of healings and miracles: all that happened in the exterior redirects us to the interior event and finds its ultimate true meaning in interiority. Let us continue to give examples, for, yet again, we are touching on a very important point.

The purified leper represents the healing of a soul that was marked by sin. Taking the parables, the one seed that becomes a great tree—that represents the birth of the kingdom in the interiority; the prodigal son was a return to interiority. We had gone to a far away country, that is, outside of ourselves, in the exteriority, neglecting God. Nicodemus, the Samaritan are both calls to discover the interiority. The great commandment—that which should distinguish a Christian, that of fraternal charity—is clearer: the other is within me. By hurting him, I hurt a member of the Body of Christ, thus, a part of my own body. The death/resurrection of Christ is the disappearance of the phenomenal, but an entrance into the world of interiority, into a new Life. That is why Jesus said to his disciples: "It is good for you that I am leaving," for I will return in you through my Spirit, just like it was revealed in the sermon after the Last Supper.

Let us open our interior outlook and, in a perfect solitude with God, become conscious of what Christ brings to us: a new world, a world of interiority, which is given to us by God, for us. It is a mystery of presence. It is only perceptible in silence, because silence makes one receptive to the divine presence available. It will be filled with pure sight through which is discovered the special divine sanctuary where only God is with it and with those he loves. "Those who love me will keep my word, and my Father will love them, and we will come to them and make our home with them" (Jn 14:23).

Let us hear the promises Christ made to those who work to keep his commandments, promises which he burned to realize in each of us: "On that day you will know that I am in my Father, and you in me, and I in you. They who have my commandments and keep them are those who love me; and those who love me will be loved by my Father, and I will love them and reveal myself to them" (Jn 14:20–21).

That is the goal that we must envision right from the beginning of the spiritual life, for that is the desire and the will of the Lord. It is not to lift the beings towards an impossible ideal, but to make them enter into a kingdom of interiority. There is no deep spiritual life, nor true spiritual fruitfulness, outside of this life of union with our Lord: "Abide in me as I abide in you. Just as the branch cannot bear fruit by itself unless it abides in the vine, neither can you unless you abide in me" (Jn 15:4).

Eternal life begins down here because of interiority: "And this is eternal life, that they may know you, the only true God, and Jesus Christ whom you have sent" (Jn 17:3). Then our heart will understand a bit of what Saint John's Christ means: "that they may all be one. As you, Father, are in me and I am in you, may they also be in us...that they may become completely one, so that the world may know that you have sent me and have loved them even as you have loved me" (Jn 17:21, 23).

This introduction to interiority is not original to Eckhart, but is destined to make his thoughts better understood, for it is man who has the passion for unity. The interior man is a noble man, a man of unification, and a man of unity.

THE WAY

Christ is the one who reveals interiority, the way that leads from exteriority to interiority (see Jn 14:6). That is the great light that must shine on our entire being, our life, all of this retreat.

And Christ tells us that we have a Father and he will lead us to him.

All souls yearn for the light. It shone in the darkness. Yet the soul has the capacity for light insomuch as it is an image of God, for it is said in the Book of Genesis: "Then God said, 'Let us make humankind in our image, according to our likeness...'" (1:26).

In the soul's progression towards the light, it must rediscover that resemblance since the image is never lost. Also, the soul will become luminous by uniting itself with the light.

> When the soul takes refuge in the knowledge of the real truth, in the power where we recognize God, then the soul can call itself light (AM, Sermon "Consideravit semitas domus tuae," p. 218).

But the soul must lean towards the light, in the same way a flower leans towards the sun, before having the power to become the light.

Saint John said that God is light. This light becomes visible and shines in certain hearts. The Word is the true light and it is like a light that the Word came to live amongst us. He is the true light. It was not a reflection like with Moses or John the Baptist, but it was the very splendor of God who came all the way to us.

The Logos, the only son of God, took on a body and became Christ so that man would return to God [= the One], in and through him. He was born, once, in Bethlehem, but like Origen already said: "what is his birth in the manger to me if he wasn't born in me into the manger of my heart?"

"For God so loved the world that he gave his only Son, so that everyone who believes in him may not perish but may have eternal life" (Jn 3:16).

Why did God make himself become a man?

Precisely in order to be born into our hearts and thus edify us. Eckhart said:

> so that I would be engendered like this same God (JAH, Sermon 29, "Convescens praecipit eis," p. 239).

That is what prepares us to tackle the basis of the entire spirituality of the Master of Cologne: the birth of God in the soul.

REFLECTION QUESTIONS

How do I respond to the light of Jesus Christ in my life? Do I
allow it to guide me and direct the decisions and paths I choose?
Or do I sometimes block out this light with distractions and
concerns that are less than what God wants for me? How can
I allow the light of God to shine through me in my daily life?
Might daily Scripture readings help in the endeavor to internalize the Word of God so that it transforms me?

DAY THREE

Birth

___

FOCUS POINT

Christ is born in us and we are to nurture our relationship with him. This birth of Christ allows us to participate in the Divine; in this way, mankind is united with God after being separated from him for so long by original sin. Christ's birth in us is the great gift of God to his creation; it comes about through God's great love for us. It also calls on us to reciprocate in our own way, to devote our will to loving he who loved us first. We can love God in our prayer and in our service to others.

___

To the one who would ask me: why do we pray, why do we fast, why do we do all of our good works, why are we baptized, why did God become man, which was the most sub-

lime? I would reply: so that God is born into the soul and the soul is born into God. It is for that reason that the Scriptures are written, that is why God created the world...so that God is born into the soul and the soul is born in God (JAH, Sermon 38, "Missus est," p. 48).

───────

HE IS BORN IN US

For all eternity, the Father engenders the Son, his alter ego, his perfect image. He did not engender him any other time; this action happened in an eternal present, it now perpetuates itself; continuously the Father engenders the Son. And this divine and co-eternal Son is contemplated by the Father; the Son loves the Father and, by this loving gaze that they exchange in the simplicity of the divine essence, the Father and the Word, like a single principle, create the Holy Spirit.

God is Birth because he is the Trinity.

This divine life which will be the substance of our heavenly happiness already communicates itself to our souls, on the condition that we are in a state of grace.

Have we thought about these sublime truths?

Let us stop to meditate on them.

He is constantly born in us.

Each soul attracts and welcomes the Word into itself according to its capacity and faith, for he wants to realize the mystery of his incarnation in all people, but not in a hypostatic way. To receive the Word (see Jn 1:12) is to allow him to come into us to the point that he takes total possession of our being.

To be born of God (see Jn 1:13) remains a hidden mystery in the majority of people. They are "the children of God" without "realizing" what that really means. Baptism initiates this birth and the Eucharist—the sacrament of unity—develops it, thus the subject always becomes more "a child of God." What we are, the Son, we have to become. That is the great light of this pilgrimage towards the Absolute [= our life] on which we will meditate. It will become a veritable odyssey, where the soul, little by little, realizes that this eternal birth fulfills itself within itself.

God is an active birth of himself and of the other (mankind) in him.

It is to this birth of God in us—the engendering of the Word in our hearts, the coming of the three divine Persons into the depth of the soul, the regeneration of our being through grace—that we will come back to during our day.

To participate in this birth is to participate in the Ultimate.

God's most noble desire is to create. He is not satisfied until he engenders his Son in us. In the same way, the soul is never satisfied if the Son of God is not born within it (JAH, Sermon 11, "Impletum est tempus Elizabeth," p. 115).

To help our prayers, we consult the Prologue to the Gospel of John (1:12): "But to all who received him, who believed in his name, he gave power to become children of God," that is, to become, through grace, through filial adoption, that which the only Son was through his eternal birth, by transferring the grace to man, created in God's image, a participation in the divine being.

The Second Letter of Peter (1:4) says the same thing: "...so that through them you may escape from the corruption that is in the world...and may become participants of the divine nature."

Saint Paul's texts abound: "and if we are children, the heirs, heirs of God and joint heirs with Christ (Rom 8:17); "Now you are the body of Christ and individually members of it" (1 Cor 12:27); and it is even more startling in: "for in Christ Jesus you are all children of God through faith. As many of you as were baptized into Christ have clothed yourselves with Christ" (Gal 3:26–27); "You are no longer a slave but a child, and if a child then also an heir, through God" (Gal 4:7); and finally: "and it is no longer I who live, but it is Christ who lives in me" (Gal 2:20); "See what love the Father has given us, that we should be called children of God; and that is what we are...we are God's children now; what we will be has not yet been revealed" (1 Jn 3:1–2).

We could easily multiply the citations.

We have the scriptural foundation of Eckhart's great theme: the birth of God in the soul.

We know this verse of the Gospel: "While he (Jesus) was saying this, a woman in the crowd raised her voice and said to him, 'Blessed is the womb that bore you and the breasts that nursed you!' But he said: 'Blessed rather are those who hear the word of God and obey it!'" (Lk 11:27).

This is what Eckhart, with his taste for excesses, had to say:

> God preferred to have been spiritually born of each virgin, of each virtuous soul, rather than to have been corporally born of Mary (JAH, Sermon 22, "Ave, gratia plena," p. 192).

For:

As truly as, in his simple nature, the Father naturally engendered his Son, he also engendered him in the most intimate part of the spirit, and there lies the interior world (JAH, Sermon 5b, "In hoc apparuit," p. 78).

THE GIFT

If we do not give God his due as God, we interrupt the movement of God, his life in the soul. If he is a gift, he is an integral gift. Could God give himself in portions, in small pieces? But he is only a gift if we are in the act of receiving. If there is no reciprocity of the gift, there is no relationship.

God is a gift. If he could not give, we kill him in us, that is, he could not show himself as being alive to us. In fact, we are given to ourselves through the gift of the Son—son within the Son: the gift is so perfect, the gift of all gifts.

His way of giving is to engender his Son. To work to reciprocate that gift to the giver is to participate in the life of the Holy Spirit.

There is, then, only one celebration for man: the existence of God.

In the instant that we reach eternity, time is abolished through the birth of God within us.

Thus, it takes more than a birth of the soul in God, but a birth of God in the soul.

A son is not a son without a father.

A father is not a father without a son.

His joy is that you make him the Father.

How?

By reciprocating his gift, by reciprocating the gift to the giver and that is an act of thanksgiving.

The reciprocation of the gift that is made in Christ is not

made by Christ alone; he does it with all of his brothers, that is, with all of himself, for it is not all of him without us.

But:

> To be born means to become: for the soul to become, it is through its eternal birth.... It becomes so totally one that there remains no other distinction than this: (if) it abides in God, it abides in the soul (MSH, Sermon, "Nisi granum frumenti," p. 131).

Also, to be contemplative, is, in inner solitude, to receive the divine Word, to conceive of it spiritually and to have nothing more than one single life with him.

> He engenders himself in us so that he will have all of his joy in the soul and that we will have all of our joy in him (JAH, Sermon 59, "Daniel...sprichet," p. 194).

REFLECTION QUESTIONS

If "to be born means to become," then how is Christ "becoming" in me? Do I devote appropriate time in my life to dwelling with Jesus Christ, who is born in my interior? Where is that quiet place in my life where I can go and give myself totally to him in silence and in solitude? How can I find time in my schedule to "make time" for this spiritual relationship, the nourishment of my soul? What activities that do not nourish me can I remove from my current schedule?

DAY FOUR

Detachment

FOCUS POINT

"God gives of himself in the same amount as we welcome him."
And we welcome God by opening ourselves totally to him.
This means freeing ourselves from those attachments that keep
us from giving ourselves completely to God. Any attachment
in our lives (be it something material—like money—or something emotional—like pride in one's prayer life) that prevents
us from welcoming God as best we can is an attachment that
must be cut away. Detachment need not be seen as a negative
(that is, dropping those things that keep us from God), but
rather as a positive (embracing God, rising to meet him as we
cut away the strings that bind us down).

You possess as much as you are detached. I would have as much as I give up.... When is God your God? When you aspire to nothing else, for that is when you have a taste for God (JAH, Sermon 74, "Dilectus Deo et hominibus," p. 98).

When an artist makes a statue, he adds nothing to the wood. He removes something from it, using his tools, he removes all of the exterior...and then what can be found hidden inside can shine (Tractate 108, cited in Michel Henry: "The essence of the manifestation," volume 1, p. 395).

RENUNCIATION DOESN'T WORK

As we advance in our retreat, we must understand that what Eckhart suggests is very lofty and thus, in order to realize it—even just a little bit—we must try to develop a soul-like attitude: we employ the means to reach the goal. But we will utilize the means with order, care, and discernment, that is, in a way that is suitable for each of us, keeping in mind our possibilities and as a function of what the Holy Spirit suggests to each of us, for Eckhart had such a sense of the Absolute that there was no room for compromise or short-cuts.

After having seen the two conditions that were dear to Eckhart—put aside all of your worries and abandonment of self (*Gelazenheit*)—we must add a third: detachment (*Abegescheidenheit*).

Abegescheidenheit, or the stripping bare of oneself, is an important concept to Eckhart.

Gelazenheit is an abandonment in faith to this love of God, which allows us to be totally stripped bare.

These two concepts are leading to a third: the birth of God in the soul.

That is what Eckhart is all about—his essence.

The Master of Cologne also took care to insist on the love of one's neighbor.

> I said it many times. If someone was in a state of rapture like Saint Paul and knew that a sick person was waiting for him to bring him a little soup, I would preferably tend to believe that, through love, you would leave your state of rapture and see to his needs out of a great sense of love (IS, p. 55).

All of the spiritual leaders have said and repeated this very thing. In the same way, he insisted on our detachment from what we possess. Certainly, he did not say that we shouldn't have anything, but don't be too attached to it.

AS THOUGH

Eckhart's kind of detachment is like that of Saint Paul's "as though": "...and those who buy as though they had no possessions, and those who deal with the world as though they had no dealings with it..." (1 Cor 7:30–31). Why? Because what is created becomes a sticky trap. It "catches you in its web." That is why we agree to the concessions of the day. We don't have to devalue created things, but we must put them into their proper place, or refuse to see them as the "end all and be all," the ultimate goal of our lives. The free spirit is a spirit which is close to things, but not overtaken by them. We all know that created things run the risk of becoming traps, illusions, fascinations, strictly for appearance, empty, and shallow.

What one must do, then, is to keep a distance between ourselves and created things so that we can find the axis that is the basis of all life: God.

It is clear that things are there for man's use. We must use things in our daily lives, for our own needs. If we don't, it could mean a life-or-death situation.

We must, then, release their grasp on us so that they no longer have such a hold on us. God can be "found" in everything because he is in everything, but discerning this depends on our way of looking at things: at not stopping at their materialism, but seeing their meaning and use for us, that is, we must go beyond their appearance. Then, things will not hold onto us, it will be us who have the hold on them.

We are slaves to that which alienates us. We should dominate that which is created, not be subject to it. That comes from the grandeur of the human spirit, for our hearts have been made for something greater than created things. They are created for God.

This doesn't mean that we have to reject anything.

Everything is available to us, but Eckhart wants to avoid the situation when we are mired in created things, and when we forget their relative value. He wants us to renounce using them as an ultimate end, an absolute, for if we do so, we risk the trap of wagering our happiness on them. That is not a true connection for happiness, supreme happiness.

Eckhart's kind of detachment is an exit that is an entrance. Exit, that is, a step backwards from created things. Entrance, because it coincides with the very depth of ourselves. Man, then, reaches the place of his nobleness.

Created things are a closed door to a union with God if we are stuck to them, and are their captives.

Created things are an open door to a union with God if we are free and we are the ones who dominate them.

> God is not the destroyer of any good, he fulfills. God does not destroy nature, he fulfills it. Grace does not destroy nature either, it fulfills it....
>
> Thus, we should not destroy the least good in ourselves, not a small thing in favor of a greater one, but bring it to its highest fulfillment (IS, p. 83).

Even more original still:

NO MILK, NO CHEESE
As long as God is before the soul and the soul awaits something from him, in a possessive way, it is not completely stripped bare of itself.

> Whoever loves God for his own interests, loves him like he loves his cow, for the milk and cheese it gives. This is what people always do who love God for exterior wealth or interior consolation, they don't really love God, they love what they can get from him (JAH, Sermon 16b, "Quasi vas auri solidum," p. 151).

"VIRGIN-LIKE" INTELLECT
Desires, spiritual pleasures, and consolations could be obstacles and mire us within ourselves. The soul unites with God when it no longer works towards reaching him. Thus, Eckhart wanted to establish the soul in a state of total bareness in order to lead it to a "virgin-like" intellect, that is, pure and free of discur-

sive thoughts: to remove all images, disencumber it of all forms and silence the conceptual within us. We are all familiar with this quotation from a Muslim mystic: "Cut off your head and you will be able to enter into the sanctuary," which, surely means: stop speaking and then you will enter into the sanctuary, that is, the place where God dwells. The goal of this stripping bare of self is so that the intellect will not hinder the elevation of the Divine in the soul.

AVAILABILITY

Attachment prevents you from being available to God. Making it a plan, a project, a personal project, removes your availability to God. We must leave God free to totally invest in man.

DISAPPROPRIATION

A Hail Mary said when man is totally divested of himself is more profitable than a thousand psalms recited without it. Even making a step in the direction of this means more than having crossed the sea [having done a very great thing] without it (IS, p. 58).

SIN

Eckhart defines sin as: concrete negative things, or illogical actions in our own interest. This is how he recommends treating them: give them to God and God will manifest himself in them if they are regretted and give mercy.

The more we judge our sin as being serious, the more God is disposed to pardon the sin, to come to the soul and chase away the sin, each having the greater zeal to suppress that which is contrary to God. The greater the number and seriousness, the more God loves to pardon them endlessly and as quickly as they are contrary to him. And when repentance lifts itself towards God, all sins disappear into God's abyss quicker than the blink of an eye and, then, they are absolutely destroyed, it is as if they had never been committed, as long as the repentance is total (IS, p. 62).

LOSS OF CONFIDENCE IN ONE'S SELF IN ORDER TO BRING IT TO GOD.

We recognize true and perfect love by the great hope and trust we have in God, for there is nothing that can give more proof of perfect love than trust....

Man could never have too much trust in God.

For all who have had great trust in him like this, he never lacked fulfilling great things (IS, p. 62).

The faithful God often allows his friends to succumb to their weaknesses so that they will no longer have any help towards which they could turn or lean on.... He removes support from them so that he can be their only support...for the more stripped bare a spirit that comes to God is, who is supported by him, the more man is profoundly fixed in God, and the more sensitive he is to God's most precious gifts, for man must build on nothing except God alone (IS, p. 71).

DIVESTING OF HIS WORKS

We must also detach ourselves from our good acts, for it is another One who is the origin of them. Detachment is, thus, a liberation of self, an opening to God, who is the depth of all beings.

> Humility of spirit occurs when man accords and attributes all of the good that has been done to God, even though God never actually did anything (JAH, Sermon 49, "Beatus venter," p. 125).

RENUNCIATION TO ONE'S SELF

> You must abandon yourself totally, then that is true abandonment. A man came to see me a short time ago and told me that he had abandoned his greatest possessions, land and goods, in order to save his soul. I then thought: Oh! How few and insignificant are the things you have abandoned! It is always a type of blindness and foolishness when you consider what you have abandoned. You have truly abandoned something when you have abandoned yourself (JAH, Sermon 28, "Ego elegi vos de mundo," p. 232).

There are two types of "me" in us. It is necessary to abandon the little egoist me in order to receive the great me, the Christlike me. "It is no longer I who live, but it is Christ who lives in me" (Gal 2:20).

Renunciation is to make the small me die so that the great me develops, grows, and invades all of what is within us. The substitution of one me for the other is an exit that is an entrance: the exit of the old person, the entrance of the new one.

INDIFFERENCE

A detached person is as sick as he is well. He loses an eye, he is not angry: he knows that he is the son of God.

This has nothing to do with stoic apathy, for the loss of health is a way by which God comes.

> Love God as freely in poverty as in wealth, love him as well in illness as in good health, as well in temptation as in none, love him as well in suffering as in none (JAH, Sermon 30, "Praedica verbum," p. 246).

HE GIVES

The kind of detachment advocated by Eckhart scares us, but detachment is identically discovered in both the depth of the soul and in God. It progresses and grows.

> Someone who has a vision of what he will have in exchange has not left everything. Moreover, he still doesn't know: "what no eye has seen, nor ear heard, nor the human heart conceived, what God has prepared for those who love him" (1 Cor 2:9).
>
> In my opinion, I praise detachment more than any kind of love. For this reason: what is best about love is that it forces me to love God, but detachment forces God to love me. It is nobler to force God to come to me than force me to go to him because God can more intimately insert himself into me and better unite with me than I could unite with him. May detachment force God to come to me, I prove it in this way: everything likes to be in the place that is proper and natural to it. The proper and natural place for God is unity and pu-

rity, and that is what detachment produces. Therefore, it is necessary for God to give himself to a detached heart (D, pp. 160–161).

We must rid ourselves of the idea that the spiritual life is a conquest or an acquisition. No, it is a stripping bare, a liberating stripping. We are connected, but Christ comes to break that connection in order to make an alliance with us, one with him.

What is called for is a step back, a distancing from the sensory surface in order to reach interiority. All of the layers covering the soul, the superimpositions, prevent us from reaching its depth.

What we must remember is that God gives of himself in the same amount as we welcome him.

Detachment is the negative side: to be one with the bottom, the positive side of the same reality.

Also, as much as there is detachment, there is God being born in the soul.

The two are correlated.

If we detach ourselves from ourselves, he will fulfill us. That is why denunciation is not a taking, but a giving.

If we have the impression that he is taking, it is because we are at the surface of ourselves, but God only works in simple hearts which are stripped bare, without attachments.

Let us finish this day with a quotation that Eckhart loved:

To be empty [effectively] of all creatures, is to be filled with God,

   To be filled [effectively] with all creatures, is to be void of God (D, p. 164).

REFLECTION QUESTIONS

Many times in my life, attachments which keep me from opening myself totally to God as best as I can are not apparent to me. Who in my life (a trusted friend, a spouse, a spiritual director) can I turn to for feedback in this regard? How often do I find myself relying on various attachments (money, pride, and so on) when, in reality, God is enough for me? Do I see detachment as a negative (having to give up habits) or as a positive (reaching for God, and cutting away all strings that keep me from his total love)?

DAY FIVE

Without Asking Why

FOCUS POINT

God knows what is best for each one of us. He knows us better than we know ourselves. This is why we must seek him rather than ourselves. Our happiness lies in him and his plan, not in ours. God is the ultimate end to our existence, the joy of eternity in peace and love. God is why we serve God. There is no other motive, no other reason worthy of our service to God. God gives himself to us; we give ourselves back to God. It is as simple as that. There is no need to ask "why?"

Know this: as long as, in one way or another, you seek what is good for you, you will never find God, because you are not exclusively seeking God. You seek something else at the same time as you seek God and it is exactly as if you treat God as a light by which you seek something and once you find what you seek, you throw the light away. You act like this because that which you seek at the same time as God is nothing, you seek nothing, that is why you find nothing....

But he who seeks without knowing why, receives, from God, all that he possesses as he possesses it (JAH, Sermon, "Omne datum," p. 65–66).

GRATUITOUSNESS

This effort of detachment, well understood and modulated for each person, on which we have reflected, should bring us great spiritual freedom. We will, then, be careful to allow things to come to us. This attitude is perhaps not much different from that which is recommended by Zen or Graf Durckheim (he recognizes Eckhart as his Master). Allow things to happen to us by themselves because we are the center of the lines of the forces of Providence. But that requires great faith and abandonment, about which we have already spoken.

Man seeks God "for" his utility. Don't make God a "milk cow," Eckhart tells us, he will fulfill us with more than just milk. His good is himself.

Certainly, he is the dispenser of all goods, but Eckhart didn't like the "I give so that you will give me in return" mentality. In Sermon 1, "Intravit Jesus in templum," he explains that the temple is not the one in Jerusalem, but the one in the soul. We must empty the temple, chase the merchants away, if not the sense of mercantilism, then the procedure of exchange: I give you this, give me that in return. But, we never give anything to God. He wants to make us enter into a perspective that is higher, that of gratuitousness, that of the honor and glory of God. In the same way as Christ received everything from the Father, he invites us to be purely receptive; for that, we must empty the soul. This emptying ensures that we will be able to receive our self from God. That is a point on which we should stop and meditate. Expect nothing in exchange, but know that we will be fulfilled, for to receive oneself from God is to be engendered by God. God is a gift.

We reconstruct the gift, then we are gifts ourselves. The soul is just a place of passage or exchange for God with himself. To an abundant source of water, one must take an empty vase, where the emptiness is not a refusal of things, but an acceptance of freeing distance. It is the welcome to the gift that produces the return-gift. To reciprocate the gift of God is an act of thanksgiving. God's gift calls for a reciprocation, a recognition, for the gift is a total one. It is a recognition that becomes fruitful, for it is God's nature to be giving. His way of giving is to engender his Son. We are given to ourselves through the gift of his Son: son in the Son, such is the perfect gift.

In effect, Christ is never alone. He is not complete without us, we have already said that. We must always think of him with all mankind, for he must reach out to cover everything and to form his Mystical Body. With him, we must build the other part of himself: his Body, for God has instituted the total Christ (= head and body). The beloved Son of the Father is Christ, Mary's son as well, but he also has a number of brothers, us in Christ. Son in the Son, but that makes only one, single Christ. What is needed is a conquest of the Christlike conscience.

In the depth of the soul, there are no other questions, we are in the state of "without whys." We live without consoling justifications, free. In order to reach Jerusalem, one must always pass by Samaria.

Only those who seek God will find God.

To seek without asking why is to discover the unique why behind everything: "God is the truth of the true and the life of the living."

No longer ask the reason why, the answer will always be found in one, single word: God.

THE CERTAINTY OF BEING FULFILLED

God is held to nothing, so don't seek to buy him. Do not be merchants, but know that if we serve him with gratitude, for his honor and glory, then:

> Jesus will reveal himself with a gentleness and infinite bounty that will flow from the strength of the Holy Spirit and overflow and flow with a bounty and a rich and super-abundant sweetness in all receptive hearts. When Jesus reveals himself with this bounty and this sweetness and unites himself to the soul, the soul floods back with this bounty and this sweetness in itself, outside of itself, and beyond itself in all things (JAH, Sermon 1, "Intravit Jesus in templum," p. 49).

"Without asking why" is to gratuitously serve. But in it, this immediately conquers itself with God and the separating duality of conscience between God and man disappears. Above all, we will meditate on the meaning of gratuitousness in our actions and in our connections with God.

We will develop our faith in the certainty of being fulfilled in this way. It is by rendering justice (= what is due to God) to God that we will have the Life. The connection with justice is the connection to truth. The connection with truth is the connection to the Life.

The more we seek you, the less we will find you.

But if you do not seek him, you will find him (JAH,
Sermon 15, "Homo quidam nobilis," p. 143).

Without asking why, because all interested motives must be
banished.

We must give ourselves up to divine freedom, but know
that the movement of interiority produces meaning, for: without asking why will be to discover the unique why of all things,
to know God who gives meaning to everything.

If you seek God alone, you will find, at the same time,
all that God has to offer to you (JAH, Sermon 26,
"Mulier, venit hora," p. 220).

All things have a why, but God doesn't have a why,
and the person who asks God for anything other than
himself, makes God become a "why" (JAH, Sermon
59, "Daniel...sprichet," p. 193).

REFLECTION QUESTIONS

When I am serving God, doing a good deed, how aware am I
of my motivation for this action? Do I see this good deed I am
doing as a "point made in heaven," or do I serve and do good
deeds without asking "why"? If I am one who asks "why?"
how can I get into the habit of service and love that asks no
questions and has no conditions? God will grace me with this
selfless love if I ask for it and continue to love and serve until
it becomes second nature.

DAY SIX

The Depth of the Soul

FOCUS POINT

In our prayer lives, in our faith lives, we must never seek ourselves. We must forget ourselves, abandon our wills, and allow Christ within our souls to take over. More precisely, our wills must be united with God's so that his plan will be the one that we follow. We must explore the depths of our soul and, finding God there, we must secure ourselves to him, for he is the source and summit of all joy and peace.

Moses said: "the one who is sent me," the one who is without a name, a negation of all names, and who never had a name [a name encloses the being, distinguishes him from others, qualifies him]. That is why the prophet said: "In truth, you are the hidden God," at the depth of the soul (JAH, Sermon 15, "Homo quidam nobilis, pp. 142–143).

THE PLACE OF THE SUPREME

In order to truly be myself at the very center of myself, I must make the little me exit in order to have an entrance of the great me, the true me, Christ's own me. To leave is then to enter. With interiority, then, there is a constant movement and action: that of returning to the source of our thoughts and actions. The whistle that calls us comes from the innermost depths, the summit of the soul, the spark, the strong fortress, the place of coincidence, of unity. The more closely man approaches it, the more he is man. There is no static possession of God, but what is perceived about God, from the depths, is thrown even further into the depths. The adventure of the spirit is, then, to come back to the center.

> I spoke of a power in the soul [in fact, there is not a power, that is not really his thought, but he lacked the proper term]; in its first burst, it doesn't grasp God because of the fact that he is good; it doesn't grasp God because of the fact that he is the truth; it penetrates and continues to seek and grasp God in his unity and solitude; it grasps God in his desert and in his own depth. That is why it is satisfied with nothing and continues to seek what God is in his deity and in the particularity of his own nature (JAH, Sermon 10, "In diebus suis placuit Deo," p. 111).

We must, then, dig deeply in order to reach the Supreme's place within us, the place where God dwells, in order to dwell in God's place. That presupposes an evangelization of all of the structures of our being: sensations, will, imagination, intellect…. What it takes, then, is a return to the place of our origins, a voyage towards the place of unity, so that we are in dispersion, but such is the true history of man.

God is also God through the action by which he became man. God is God (= he remains God) in this movement of transition, in the desire to be the other, without stopping to be himself. The movement of the divine persons in the Holy Trinity is his being and the distinctive feature of his freedom. But his movement freely reaches out and it is also what he is trying to do, to become "us." It is, then, the being of God (= love), himself, in this movement of transition towards an "otherness." By making himself a man, God affirms himself (to man's eyes) as God. It is by expressing himself like the other of himself that he affirms what he is for us: a gift.

What is needed is not a fusion, but an expanding unity, a unity in the midst of producing a rational otherness. God is the one who is pouring out his heart and he does so where he finds a place for it, that is, where there are no obstacles. What is needed, then, is a unity within a duality. God is both the end and the beginning (= always new). But we can only aim at this dual unity through resemblance. Genesis tells us that man was created in the image and likeness of God. Let us remember that the image is inalienable, but it is as if it is at the bottom of a well that has been obstructed by sin. The resemblance isn't there, it can't exist there and when it exists, it is quite variable as are souls.

God, in his Christ, leads us to this place of truth which is at the depth of the soul. That is the place of the ultimate since it is the one with the depth of God, in the sense that the depth of the soul is deep and emerges as God. The center of the soul is God. That is on what we should always meditate. Yes, we must always return to this great truth. When this single place is reached, it is peace.

Many people do not know that they have a heart, they don't know their hearts. The return to the heart—the "redi ad cor" of Saint Augustine—is the fruit of grace and not only as a result of man's efforts. This must suffice to distinguish Asiatic spiritualities or pseudo-spiritualities. The heart is the point where man is in contact with God. Only faithfulness in prayer can lead there. It is an extremely simple point. It is the goal of our being to be united to God, acting with God. Our being has become "virginal," that is, without discursive thoughts. It is the fruit of detachment and an availability to God, more than of an effort of concentration.

THE PLACE OF COMMUNION

When I pray for someone, it is the most minimal prayer. When I pray for no one [= without mentioning any particular intentions] and I ask nothing [= for myself], I most truly pray (JAH, Sermon 65, "Deus caritas est," p. 38).

Eckhart also explains himself in another passage:

I want to explain to you how I think about another person: I work at forgetting myself, then in the same way, all humans and, for them, I enter into the Unity (JAH, Sermon 64, "Die sele die wirt," p. 33).

It is in the search for the divine union that the soul effectively finds its brothers. At each moment, it operates in each of us in an invisible, but very real, way and enriches us, by virtue of the communion of the saints, and the divine life that is takes from the wellspring of its source. It comforts the world since it has no worries except God and unity. "Those who abide in me and I in them bear much fruit, because apart from me you can do nothing" (Jn 15:5).

The soul, then, doesn't save itself alone, it brings with it all of those who seek God and all of those whom God seeks. Its effectiveness, intercession, and brilliance depend upon the reality and the intensity of its intimate union with the Lord.

If I am fixed on God, I could not help but participate in his work of sanctification of the world. Also, through detachment, the soul totally trusts God for the fulfillment of its prayer, for a certain intention. This reliance on God avoids multiplicity, dispersion of spiritual attention, and this act of abandonment does not disturb the solitude with God, it assures it. Through our act of forgetting ourselves, we find ourselves again in God, for it is in him, alone, that creatures can meet and truly unite.

Also, the best prayer that man could make isn't to say:

"Give me this virtue or this manner of being or: Lord, give yourself to me, or give me eternal life,"

but to truly say: "Lord, give me only what you want to and Lord, make of me what you want and in the way you want to do it."

This prayer surpasses all others in such a way that heaven will dominate the earth (IS, p. 42).

REFLECTION QUESTIONS

Am I determined to forget myself in my spiritual life? How does one do this? Might I offer the prayer that Meister Eckhart suggests above? When I forget myself, and my will is removed from my prayer life, at what place will I find my faith life? Do I rely on God totally in my life? What areas of my life might need more of a detachment from what is less than God and more of an attachment to that which is God?

DAY SEVEN

The Search for the Model

FOCUS POINT

The model of the perfect relationship between man and God is the man-God, Jesus Christ. As a man, Jesus taught us that we are not alone, that God is always with us, united to us. We are to nourish and deepen this unity throughout our lives. In this deepening relationship, this unity of our will with that of the Divine, interior silence is key to our discovery of who we are in God.

The prototype of the soul...is the Son. He is the model for all creatures and the image of the Father, the prototype where all of the essence of all creatures is in suspension (AM, "How the soul follows its own path and finds itself," p. 248).

The Father recognizes himself for all eternity in his Word, in the Son. At the same time as the Father expresses himself in him, he perceives the ideal reasons for things, the ideal being, the prototype, the model for all possible creatures. Their example can all be found in the Word, their virtual existence. He is the model that the artist conceived in his thoughts. We meditate on these terms because, in order to find his Christ there, and, for this unique goal alone, the Father created man; it is Christ he seeks in humanity, his own identical image, his Word. Does he not want to engender us in him and glorify him in us?

Creation in time makes certain of these possible beings pass from the universe of eternal "intra divine" beings to the universe of the phenomenal being, the one of our time-space reality. Creation, then, situates man in multiplicity and place at a point that is the farthest from unity. The whole reason behind time, then, is to allow man to return to his element. In order for that to happen, he must reunite with his prototype at his deepest point. That procedure is introversion, which is very dear to people like Eckhart.

FOR THE PRAISE AND GLORY OF HIS GRACE

In this perspective of exemplary nature, a creature will be even more itself, more conformed to its goal, that it will "stick" closer to the divine idea that gave form to its creation. This idea is not something from the soul, but it is in the soul, *distinct* from it, but still "attached" to it at its depth and it pushes man, helped by grace, to get back to its source.

The prototype is a differentiating expression from unity.

What do we do in order to get back to our source?

We must realize the idea that God had for us for all eternity. It would be good here to bring to mind the beginning of Saint Paul's Letter to the Ephesians (1:3–10): "Blessed be the God and Father of our Lord Jesus Christ, who has blessed us in Christ with every spiritual blessing in heavenly places, just as he chose us in Christ before the foundation of the world to be holy and blameless before him in love. He destined us for adoption as his children through Jesus Christ, according to the good pleasure of his will, to the praise of his glorious grace that he freely bestowed on us in the Beloved. In him we have redemption through his blood, the forgiveness of our trespasses, according to the riches of his grace...he has made known to the mystery of his will, according to his good pleasure that he set forth in Christ...to gather up all things in him, Christ."

In order to get back to our prototype, we must, first of all, discover our vocation.

To discover our vocation is to construct our self; it is to discover a level that is even deeper in our being.

Prototype and vocation are connected just like the end is to the means used to reach it.

To realize this vocation is to realize oneself, and to do that is to fulfill one's life.

Right from the time we begin our true vocation, it appears that God is with us, watching over us. We are full of confidence and joy for we lose the feeling of being abandoned. All discoveries of vocations are annunciations.

Man is born in many ways. He has fulfilled his life if he dies united. An obstacle to our vocation, the idea that God has for us by creating us, is dispersion, the distancing from the center, that is, a failure to reach the unity sought (= sin, negativity).

The prototype is the Word. In him, God reserves a vocation for each of us in order to return to unity, a vocation that is singular, unique, and different for each of us.

That is why it comes from far away, from a place that is beyond ourselves and we feel that it has passed through us and overwhelmed us.

With the pieces of our being and our life, our vocation puts the pieces of the puzzle that we are together.

In order to discover, live, and realize our vocation as baptized members, silence, which allows the profound grasp of our being, is necessary. Also, if we want rejoin God's idea of himself and then conform to it, silence is essential, for it is in this way that we can be attentive to what happens with him, by him, and around him.

There are sometimes errors in interpretation and we may, at times, find ourselves far from being connected. Today, we will also meditate mainly on the text of Paul's Letter to the Ephesians, cited on page 47.

EVERYTHING DEPENDS UPON THE UNION OF WILL

In order to come back to our prototype, we must not only discover our vocation, but make an effort to always adhere to God's will for us.

We believe that we must realize "May I do your will," but it's not like that. "Do your will in me" is much better. To accept, in all circumstances, in the most generous way possible, the will of God for us, that is the great means to come back to our origin (= prototype), in order to be what we are in that prototype. Also, let us allow God to do his will in us, let us allow God to be what he wants to be in us.

Man could not want what he wants (in his very depth) on

his own, and he could not realize it with his own forces. What he achieves is not enough to satisfy a desire that he could only arrive at in silence.

Also, anyone who puts his end in the finite, who "absolutizes" what is relative, is lost, for he has not followed his interior desire which steers him towards the divine infinite that is calling him. To want to enclose oneself in one's own limitations and reduce one's desires is to wish for negativity. But we move according to the transcendent call which no longer pacifies desire, much to the contrary. That makes us vividly feel a discrepancy between what we tend to be and what we are. To look closely at this desire is to look deeply at the capacity of the gift and the capacity for welcome. It permits us to concretely discover, in the midst of all the contradictions of life, the meaning that we want to give to the realization that God awaits from us by decoding the signs that he gives us.

Something in me is hungry and thirsty, I feel a void that is not fulfilled, it is the "vacuum" that will permit me to go even more towards my prototype. That will be a crossing of a desert, of a sterile soil, of the opacity of my being, but I will walk towards the promised land, for I believe that Christ is the revelation of my prototype.

By exploring the mirror of his soul, man will discover his eternal face: that which he is in God.

> Those who want something other than the will of God will get what they deserve. They are always unhappy and in distress…. It is justified. They love God for something other than what God is (MSH, Sermon, "Beati qui esuriunt," p. 190).

And they will miss their prototype. We will learn to know how to discover, adore, and love the divine will at the basis of whatever happens to us for, then, the soul will become what God wants it to be.

The soul can never find rest before uniting with the idea that God has for each one of us in his eternity.

REFLECTION QUESTIONS

In order to learn more about the model for human-divine relationships—Jesus Christ—what avenues other than prayer do I explore? Do I attend Mass on a regular basis so that I might hear Christ's words proclaimed in the Gospel and hear him spoken of in the homily? Do I practice spiritual reading independent of the Mass, reading the works of Fathers or Doctors of the Church, biblical commentaries, or other works?

DAY EIGHT

The Image

FOCUS POINT

We are created in the image of God, and when we are free from attachments God's image in us shines through for all to see. When we are detached from those habits and ways of thinking that tie our spirit down, keeping it from God, we are transformed by the image of God inside us. We must seek to dwell in the mystery of the Incarnation if we are to deepen our love relationship with God and truly resemble him in all that we are and all that we do.

Let us take a basin that is filled with water, place a mirror in it and leave it out in the sun. The sun will equally project its vivid brilliance all the way to the bottom of the basin and not just the image of its circular shape and this brilliance has not been weakened in any way. The reflection of the mirror exposed to the sun, just like it does in the sun, can be truthfully said to be equal to the sun, and the mirror, nonetheless, remains what it is. It is the same way with God. God is in the soul with his nature, with his essence, and his deity, and yet he is not the soul. The reflection of the soul that operates in God is, properly speaking, equally God and, nonetheless, it remains what it is (AM, Sermon, "Nolite timere eso," p. 245).

AN ADJECTIVE TO THE WORD

Why must we disencumber the mental, conform to the will of God, empty ourselves, liberate ourselves, and return to the virginity of the soul? So that the image of God shines in our depth.

We must take care to note that the will of God is not some type of information that we must intercept by waves that he sends to us; it is the willing will (as opposed to what we desire). The willing will is a profound will, the fundamental will, the ultimate desire. It is the will that is concretely carried out by the interior thrust.

The depth is the place where each of the faculties must surpass themselves, the place where the strengths return to a unity.

These two points having been spelled out, we must become adjectives to the Word, the Word being the perfect image, "the image of the invisible God, the firstborn of all creation" (Col 1:15), "the reflection of God's glory and the exact imprint of God's very being" (Heb 1:3).

The Word is a movement of identification through differences. He is the expression of the Other (= the Father), his manifestation, his diction.

Adjectives: we are destined to be a word within the Word; "Ad" meaning turning towards, a relationship.

From the seed to the cob, there is a maturing, a growth. Man is God in the germinal sense. "Beloved, we are God's children now" (1 Jn 3:2).

Man is in the act of genesis.

Man will always be a child of God, that is, the one who receives the Life through grace.

When man strips himself and brings out the divine image that God created in him, the image of God is manifested in him. The more man strips and brings to clarity within himself the image of God, the clearer the birth of God is within him. The more the image is stripped, the more God shines in it.

We will, then, meditate about the image in the mirror of the soul: "And all of us, with unveiled faces, seeing the glory of the Lord as though reflected in a mirror, are being transformed into the same image from one degree of glory to another; for this comes from the Lord, the Spirit" (2 Cor 3:18); "...God who said, 'Let light shine out of the darkness,' who has shone in our hearts to give the light of the knowledge of the glory of God in the face of Jesus Christ" (2 Cor 4:6). It is the contemplation of God in Christ that makes the Christian resemble God, for "those whom he foreknew he also predestined to be conformed to the image of his Son..." (Rom 8:29).

The image, then, structures the nature of man; he must be the expression of God. Because of the image that is within each person, the movement of God is to become "us." This brings us back to Saint Augustine's famous phrase: "You made us for yourself and our hearts are unsettled as long as they don't rest in you." To rest means to be in the place of unity rather than in a place of multiplicity.

This "image" clarifies itself in the midst of the darkness in which it is plunged by God who, in Christ, in a Christlike mediation, speaks creative words. It requires a resuscitating reply which is resemblance. Alas, it is we who make this Word become constrained, but the Word is a creator, a conciliator, a savior, and divine.

Resemblance is acquired—not uniquely—through prayer. We will note that the image means a natural similarity (but one that is soiled by sin); resemblance, acquired perfection.

THE IMAGE IN THE MIRROR

Since we are sons in the Son, our prayer, united with that of the Son, will be the image of his.

However, what was Christ's prayer?

- an awareness of his most intimate consciousness about his relationship with the Father, his total dependance upon him.

- a psychological awareness that is more vivid of his filial being, a concentration of his soul at its depth where he recognizes himself as the eternal Son of God.

- the repercussion in the flesh of his relationship with the divine Person (Son) of the Father. He recognizes himself there, gives himself to the Father, more intimately to himself than himself, in a movement of thanksgiving, a movement that is his very own being.

- in brief, it was a greater and more profound actualization in his human awareness of the essential relationship that he had with the Father, of his unity

with him, with no confusion about the Persons (of
the Trinity).

However, it is said that the disciples would know the intimate relationship that the Son had with the Father through
the experience that they would have with the Son: "On that
day you will know that I am in my Father, and you in me, and
I in you" (Jn 14:20).

The Christian's prayer, then, will be an image of that of the
Son, a participation in his prayer, with respect to his Father.

To pray is to bring into consciousness what God wants me
to be: son in Jesus Christ; that is, in a relationship with the
Father, to receive everything from him, to return everything to
him through love. Love is to make what is unequal become equal.

To become a Father, doesn't one have to learn to give?

To become a Son, doesn't one have to learn to receive?

However, the heavenly Father gives all that he is, all that
he has, to his Son and, in his Son, he loves me to such a point
that, according to the Gospel, he lifts me up, he makes me
grow all the way until together, with his Son, we penetrate
into the womb of the Father (= the place of all fruitfulness).

The soul seeks to have the transparence of a smooth mirror. No longer having any shape of its own, it can reflect the
divine infinite in its entire depth. It will fix God in calmness
and contemplation. It will open its interior gaze and, in a perfect solitude with God, it will become aware of what Christ is
for it, of what God gives us, of what we reflect of that light.

It will allow God to be recognized and take pleasure in the
reflected image. The Father, flooding the soul with his love,
will see his reflection in it, which shows him the characteristics
of his Son, his "alter ego."

To be the image is to establish solitude in the soul with

God. Let us allow the Image to be reflected in our image, let it transform us. The image, under the influence of an interior gaze, which extends all the way to a place where love goes, will be channeled to the resemblance of Christ:

> May the Father and this very Word and the Holy Spirit help us to always remain "adjectives" of this same Word (JAH, Sermon 9, "Quasi stella matutina," p. 105).

REFLECTION QUESTIONS

When I look at myself in the mirror, do I see the image of God shining through? When I see myself through the eyes of the people I encounter in my daily life, do I see God's image? If not, how can I foster this image? Can I dwell on my interior image in contemplation (as Meister Eckhart suggests) of the Incarnation, that is, the unity of humankind and the Divine brought together in the person of the Son of God, Jesus Christ?

DAY NINE

Suffering

FOCUS POINT

The Incarnation must be kept in mind when we attempt to understand suffering. In the Christian context, our God understands suffering because he lived as a man. In this sense, we are united to God in a very deep way: we share in his suffering and he shares in ours. Understood like this, suffering is not as absent of God as it might seem at first, since in our suffering we are brought closer to our God, who loves us dearly and feels our suffering as much—and more—than we experience it.

Know this: if something was not the will of God, it will never be. You have no illness, no matter what, unless God wants it. And just like you know that it's the will of God, you should have so much agreement and satisfaction that you could not judge that a worry is a worry...for it belongs to God's being to want only the best (JAH, Sermon 4, "Omne datum optimum," p. 63).

Whether it is illness or poverty, or whatever God does or doesn't impose on you or give to you, all of that is the best for you (Ibid).

If you are ill and ask God for good health, your health means more to you than God: thus, he is not your God (JAH, Sermon 25, "Moyses orabat Dominum," p. 212).

GOD HANDLES OUR SUFFERING

Those are disconcerting phrases that we once again see as an example of Eckhart's excessive side! His sense of the Absolute sometimes takes him to the limits of the absurd. We would hope that he could be more moderate and reasonable, but that wouldn't be Eckhart!

Let us try to understand him, yet without following him in his excesses.

Eckhart's main idea is that suffering is always a burden, but since the Cross, it is no longer a bad thing, for that would stop the process of unity. However, since the Cross, suffering, that is, the lack of being oneself, nothingness, in a being that shouldn't have this lack, this nothingness, is transformed.

Under what conditions?

If it is God who carries the suffering.

God assumes what man agrees to abandon. Then man should not consider suffering as his, but as if it is assumed by

God. God suffers the burden of suffering, so that, for Eckhart, we suffer everything if we suffer nothing at all, for God carries it within us. Also, he invites us to rejoice in unhappiness, for we can change it into happiness, that is, in a way in order to return it to the deity.

> If someone placed a quintal (100 kg) on my back and then another person supported it, I could support a hundred as well as one alone (JAH, Sermon 2, "Intravit Jesus," p. 55).

If suffering is abandoned, that is, offered, it is God who carries the burden. That is the great idea that must accompany suffering, according to Eckhart.

Also, we must believe that, in a situation of nothingness, God could change it around and make it better for us.

We consider that God said to Job: you know nothing, you are shortsighted, give in to it, for your field of consciousness is just partial. It is for God to want what is better. It is his alone. But for us, because of our shortsightedness, it is difficult. Once again, Eckhart teaches us:

> Take note, all of you reasonable persons. The quickest vehicle that leads us to our perfection (detachment) is suffering (D, p. 171).

He wants to say that suffering with Christ is the most direct way to reach the union:

> To people, nothing disfigures the body as much as suffering, but to God, nothing embellishes the soul more than having suffered (Ibid).

Why? Because it strips me bare of myself.

> God suffers the suffering at the same time as man....
> How, in these conditions, can suffering still be a worry,
> if we lose our worries? My worries are assumed by
> God.... We know that as assuredly as God is truth;
> everywhere I find truth, I also find my God, who is the
> truth. In the same way, when I find my suffering,
> uniquely for and in God, there I find God at the place
> of my suffering! Whoever doesn't understand that, just
> has to consider his blindness and not me, nor the di-
> vine truth (LCD, ed Aubier, p. 95).

THE EXPANSION OF THE SOUL

The painful problem of the (apparent) absence of God in prayer
is resolved by Eckhart in the following way:

> If you love me, why do you pull away from me? Alas,
> Lord, you know, so that I can receive a great deal from
> you (JAH, Sermon 79, "Laudate coeli," p. 129).

There is an expansion of the welcoming capacity of the soul.
To those who lack the desire to climb to the summit, to those
who are self-satisfied, the kingdom of God is far. To those who
are poor, who have a full and painful consciousness of their
spir- itual poverty, the kingdom of heaven is near. Here, we
can see this in Sermon 52, "Beati pauperes spiritu," Eckhart's
most original sermon. But we remember that the difficulties
we encounter in prayer are resolved by just waiting for God to
make our desire grow; through this desire, he bores into the
soul, by boring into the soul, he renders it able to receive.

What must you do, then, when you sense his "departure"?

Exactly what you would do if you were in great consolation (IS, ch. 11, p. 57).

Eckhart knew the passive purifications of the soul. If they oc-
cur, the soul will accept them, for:

As large as this nothingness and lessening of self is, he
will remain imperfect if God doesn't accomplish it
within him. For humility is only truly perfect if God
humbles man by man's own hand. So only the man
really accomplishes this end (IS, ch. 23, p. 84).

Corporal death is prepared for by this detachment. It is but
the last act. I am finished and ready to die. But all during its
itinerary, life has acted as if in a sort of death, for that makes
us leave our particularity in order to reach the universal. The
"little" deaths have prepared us for the "great death" (corporal). In fact, the greatest death is that of "myself."
  In the case of suffering, for Eckhart:

God is with us during suffering, that signifies that he
suffers with us. The one who truly knows the truth
knows that what I say is true. God suffers with man,
yes, he suffers in his own way, to a greater degree and
incomparably more than the one who suffers, who suffers for him (LCD, p. 128).

This parallels what current theology seeks, but a few lines later,
he adds:

I assure you that God suffers so freely with us when
we suffer for him alone that he suffers without suffering. For him, suffering is so delectable that suffering
isn't suffering (LCD, p. 129).

Eckhart probably wants to say that suffering doesn't alter his
essential perfection, that he suffers because of his love of com-
passion.

REFLECTION QUESTIONS

How do I approach suffering in my life? Do I see it as God
being far away from me or as an opportunity to grow ever
deeper in my relationship with Jesus Christ? Can I learn anything from the life and work of Mother Teresa in this regard?
Perhaps some reading on the subject of Mother Teresa will
reveal her understanding of suffering as a way to grow in love
with God and her fellow brothers and sisters.

DAY TEN

Martha and Mary

FOCUS POINT

We find God in the present moment, the eternal present. It is in the present, where there are no lingering thoughts of the past or worries for the future, where we can be at peace with God. This place of peace in the present can be achieved apart from silence since God is with us in all that we do. We can be at work, amidst our daily life, and if we are free from worry and distraction and attachment, we can be present to and at peace with God, even during these times of activity.

Christ said to Martha: "only one thing is necessary, and not two. You and I, once we are enveloped with eternal light, become one. And [two-in-one] is an ardent spirit situated above all things and below God, surrounding all eternity" (JAH, Sermon 86, "Intravit Jesus," p. 174).

THE RETURN TO THE MARKETPLACE

Eckhart, who played such a great role in the history of spirituality, puts his emphasis not on Mary, but on Martha. How he has his feet on the ground! He values day-to-day duties, he elevates the status of our daily chores with their most menial duties, on the condition that the spirit is "free," that is, abandoned to God. From then on, no matter what action or contemplation happens, it is as if God did it. There is no longer either an interior nor an exterior. It is here that we must remember a phrase from one of Eckhart's spiritual heirs, Suso: "interiority all the way to exteriority is more interior than just interiority." So then, prayer can no longer be distinguished from work.

ECKHART'S HUMANITY!

> You think that words can always give you both joy and suffering, you are mistaken. It isn't like that.... Christ said: "you have many worries troubling you." Martha was so fulfilled that her duties didn't get in her way (Ibid, p. 177–178).

That was a return to the marketplace (business as usual), a concept which is dear to the Buddhists, busy with all of the daily duties, but freed.

NO LONGER FROM EITHER THE EXTERIOR OR THE INTERIOR

It is necessary to get back to what God asks in the present moment:

> To be with worries, but not in worries. And there, temporal work is as noble as all other assimilations to God, for it renders us as close to God as the highest elevation that could be given to us, with the single exception of the contemplation of God in the bareness of his nature (Ibid, p. 176).

Invest yourself totally in the present moment, but for and with me, this is the unique necessity.

Live the present instant for me, with me, in me, that is what is necessary.

No matter what you are doing, then, listening to my words, or stirring the gravy, what is essential is that you let me live that within you.

It is also as important to be close to things, not in them.

What is important is to be detached, thus available, ready to accept no matter what commitment I could ask of you.

Eckhart's prayers are close to our daily duties. At the basis of these jobs, what is important is to feel God's thirst, then there will no longer be either an exterior or an interior, since God can be found in everything, even in the pots and pans!

REFLECTION QUESTIONS

Am I able to be at peace with God even outside of the silent time I make for prayer with him? During the activity of my day, am I able to focus on the present moment—myself, there

with God—and avoid the attachments, concerns for the past
and future, that keep me from being present to God? How
might I go about achieving this ability to be present? Might I
consider a centering prayer (involving a sacred word or phrase)
that brings my attention back to God when I am tempted by
distraction or worry?

"Those Who Eat of Me Will Have a Greater Hunger"

FOCUS POINT

We are completely dependent on God. We are dependent on God for everything. This reality should never be lost on us. It is the source of a wonderful gratitude that wells up inside of us. Everything we have—life, family, friends, the capacity to love God and experience his great love—we owe directly to God. Our love for God grows as our souls expand, allowing more room for his love and less room for the attachments that distract us from that love.

Your hunger for God should never be satiated. God can never satiate you: the more you possess God, the more you desire him. If God could satiate you, and if you could be satiated with God, God would not be God (JAH, Sermon 83, "Renovamini...spiritu," p. 153).

"YOU ARE THE ONE WHO DOES NOT EXIST"

The commentary on Sirach 24:21 that Eckhart wrote does not aim, even in a most accommodating sense, at the Eucharist, but it is an opportunity for the Master of Cologne to show that the creatures never stop nourishing themselves with God. It comes from the dynamic context of the creative act. To eat and never be satiated, even to the point of having a greater hunger! Creatures eat, for they are; they have hunger, for they are made by an Other than themselves. Here, we will meditate on a phrase we remember that Christ said to Saint Catherine of Siena: "I exist. You are the one who does not exist." At each moment of our existence, we receive our action of existing, upon which we have a supreme dependence. A creature does not have his life, his being in himself. He receives it from God. But for Eckhart, creatures hunger for the Being. We must beg, for "the Being needs nothing, for he is lacking nothing. But the beings need him because there is nothing outside of him" (Commentary on the Book of Exodus 3:14).

Those who eat of me will still be hungry.... Me, that is to say, the One who is the Being himself. As much as we are, we are what we are only through the Being, and as such, as beings, we take our nourishment for being from him. Thus, all beings eat of God and still hunger for him.

This brings us to this assertion:

Creatures are too minuscule to reveal God (JAH, Sermon 20b, "Homo quidam fecit," p. 180).

And also: the desire for happiness is nothing other than the desire for existence. However, God makes us pass from non-existence, which is our inceptive state here below, to a state of more-existence or progressed being, which gives supernatural life.

The connection between the being and the Being, the creature and God, the adjective and the Word, that is the principle objective of Eckhart's reflection.

Thus, the creature nourishes itself with God because it is perpetually hungry for him, for it doesn't exist by itself, but takes its beginnings from God.

THE BURNING BUSH

We can also interpret this passage from Sirach in a way that is dear to the Greek Fathers, especially to Gregory of Nyssa.

The soul becomes larger through an expansion of its capacity to receive. Each new intervention by God makes it grow. It is always fulfilled by God and always in a state of wanting him even more. That is the way it is with God, and he wouldn't be God if it wasn't that way: revealing himself always more divine by increasing the participation of the soul.

"Forget what lies behind and strain forward to what lies ahead" (Phil 3:13). From this text, Saint Paul tells us that the soul doesn't stop at what it has already acquired from God. This image illustrates progress, a type of never-ending grip, and desire. No believer, even if he has made great progress, can ever say: that is enough. To have charity is to continue to grow more and more, we must always have a hunger for God. Charity increases and the soul continues to become more able to grow even greater. The more the soul goes back to the Source (God), the younger it gets.

> I would not be surprised if he would be even younger tomorrow than he is today (JAH, Sermon 42, "Adolescens, tibi dicto: surge," p. 77).

REFLECTION QUESTIONS

Do I often reflect upon how much God has given me in my life? Am I often overwhelmed by the gratitude I feel at these times? Do I recognize the never-ending love God expresses to me through those people in my life who love me and care for me and support me? How do I express my gratitude to God for all he has given me? Do I express this in prayer? Do I express this by giving of myself to others in praise of God's holy name? Do I offer up my suffering to God and unite myself with him in that way?

DAY TWELVE

The Desert

FOCUS POINT
God cannot stop from loving us. It is his nature to love us. We need not pray for his love; he gives it freely and abundantly. But God and his love are beyond our intellectual concepts, and we are left in a "desert of understanding," of not being able to understand the infinite God with our finite conceptualizing. We cross this desert by our life of faith, by knowing God's great love for us and by loving God as best we can.

I never thank God for loving me, he can't avoid it, whether he wants to or not, his nature forces him to. I thank him rather, that, in his bounty, he can't stop himself from loving me (JAH, Sermon 73, "Dilectus Deo et hominibus," p. 92).

Eckhart is a voice who cries to us: your road is a desert. From where do we come? From nothingness, but also, from our point of view, from the womb of God (exemplarism). Where are we going? Towards ourselves, but also to another point of view towards the womb of God (return to the One). Also, go on your way by letting what will be, be. What does that mean? Let God shine through everything, so that nothing other than God will shine through.

An empty soul is the place where God can function, the flame of the burning bush having consumed, in the desert of the soul, figures, concepts, in order to let the Depth (God) spring up in it from its depth and leave room for the great revelation from the desert: "I am the one who is." We will dig deeper into these words by invoking the Holy Spirit.

The person who prays with Eckhart will not discover God as an explanation of what exists or as a motivation for what he must do, nor will he find a distant God, someone from outside. No, he is *in* us.

Eckhart invites us to throw ourselves into the desert and lose ourselves there. But this desert of the virgin spirit, without images, free of all and, above all, free of oneself, leads to another desert, the one of the Deity, that is, probably of unity.

This search for the interior God makes Eckhart become a man-bridge between us and the Eastern religions. There is a narrow parallel between the spiritual void, the vacuum, the desert claimed by the Master of Cologne and the search for the Absolute of either Hinduism or Buddhism. Certainly, we don't want to make Eckhart seem to be a grandson of the Buddha, but we do want to state that we are accompanied by numerous seekers of the Absolute, both known and unknown.

In the desert, we walk with a single certainty: God's promise. That should be enough.

Look how God cherishes us, how he begs us, and God has no rest other than the soul, he turns away from no creature or rids himself of it. It is a certainty and necessary truth that God has such a need to seek us, it is exactly as if his Deity depends upon it; it is effectively so. God can no more do without us than we can do without him. Even if it would be possible that we could turn away from God, God could never turn away from us. [I say: I will not pray so that he will give me what I ask (thus I am disinterested); no more would I praise him for that which, in the past, he would have filled me. I would rather pray that he make me worthy to receive what he gives (thus I have humility) and praise him about being of such a nature and essence that he must give (thus I recognize his grandeur and what he is).] The one that would deprive God, deprives himself of his own being and of his own life (JAH, Sermon 26, "Mulier, venit hora," p. 221–222).

The glory of God is the edification of man. That is God's promise, the thing that should be the soul of our walk in the desert. And this gift is from his bounty, for he can't stop himself from loving me.

THE PURE AND BARE NOTHING
Here, the desert is the Deity (= unity).

Poem IV
This point is the mountain
to climb without acting intelligent!
The road brings you

to a marvelous desert,
to its width and breadth,
it stretches without any limits.
The desert has no
place nor time,
it has its own will (Poem, Arfuyen Editions, Paris, 1988,
p. 11).

Poem V
This desert is the Good One
trampled by no foot,
creation
has never gone there:
that is, no one
knows about it.
It is here and there,
far and near,
deep and high,
thus, in this way,
it is neither this nor that (Ibid, p. 13).

Poem VIII
Oh my soul,
Leave, God enter!
Immerse my whole being
in God who is non-being,
in this river with no end!
If I flee from you,
You come to me.
If I lose myself,
I find you,
Oh super-essential Good! (Ibid, p. 19).

These poems—*granum sinapis*; that is, wild mustard seed—are attributed to Eckhart by one of his followers, Alan of Libera. He explains that it was a work from his youth. We concur with him. We will use them for our meditation.

But in order to avoid any misunderstandings, we must provide a few explanations.

By the expression: "God who is non-being," Eckhart did not intend to make a declaration of atheism, but to the contrary, exalt him to the highest point of God's being. He is so much above being, all that we can say about him is so very little, that it returns to be non-being, nothingness, that is, outside of our intellectual categories, of which we can say nothing. It is a nothingness of transcendence and not a nothingness by default. Eckhart was careful to explain:

> When I said that God is not a being and that he is above a being, I did not deny him a sense of being; to the contrary, I attributed a more elevated being to him (JAH, Sermon 9, "Quasi stella matutina," p. 101).

In the desert, we must renounce God for God, that is, a God who listens to man, who always answers his prayers as he wishes, makes his love known to us, in which we find and take shelter. This presupposes that we join Christ in his agony at Gethsemane (the nights of Saint John of the Cross).

Then, for Eckhart, the soul that will reach God stripped bare, with no image or method, will reach the Deity.

Desert, solitude, purity, virginity—these are terms that are truly from Eckhart that we would like to meditate upon again.

What we must do is hear nothing but the eternal Word: the generation of the Word by the Father, the inspiration of Love.

It is as if these three lights become discernable in the luminous flow where, until now, we have distinguished nothing.

That is how the One operates; it is his unity. The undifferentiated divinity is not beyond but in the heart of the three Persons achieving an essential unity. Thus we can't say anything about it: it is nothingness, pure and naked, indetermination, the mystery of the divine essence.

Ergo sum qui sum: I am the One who is.

God is the being, the pure being, the very plenitude of the Being.

Eckhart gets rid of what we traditionally consider to be God's attributes: wisdom, goodness, because God is not the same kind of good as my grandfather is good. By saying that God is good, I say something about God, but I should also give no significance to this statement. God's goodness is so far beyond what can be measured, as I know how to measure it, that it totally escapes my comprehension.

God is known only in and by himself. "I am the one who is."

We can only speak of him according to our way of thinking, from the aspect of how we see things and what is known to us, even though he transcends all concepts and terms that are known to us and those we use with reference to him.

The Unity is solitary and desert-like because it bypasses all multiplicity.

He is One, pure and simple.

The desert of God is the simplicity of his essence.

No image can open either the deity or the essence of God (JAH, Sermon 76, "Videte qualem caritatem," p. 113).

REFLECTION QUESTIONS

When I attempt to express God in words, what words do I use? Do I understand that any and all words I use to describe and conceptualize God fall far short of his reality? Have I experienced the "desert of understanding"? How do I respond to this desert? Do I attempt wordless prayer, wherein I simply center myself on the reality that I am in the presence of God, totally open to his coming into me?

DAY THIRTEEN

The Opening

FOCUS POINT

In order to receive God we must make ourselves small. This is in reference to humility. We must sweep out the attachments that fill us up and open that space for God. In the Incarnation, God humbled himself for love of us, and he became man. It was this humility of his enfleshed state that allowed the greatness of the Divine to enter the finiteness, the smallness, that is man. We must humble ourselves before God and, in doing so, make ourselves receptive to his coming.

When man humbles himself, God, in his own goodness, cannot refrain from lowering himself and flowing into the humble man. It is to the smallest that he gives of himself the most and in plenitude. What God gives is his being and his being is his goodness, and his goodness is his love (JAH, Sermon 22, "Ave, gratia plena," p. 194).

S implicity (you only seek God), purity (give all the glory to God), virginity (no concepts, no images, no words), poverty (of self)—all of these lead us, little by little, to the depths.

That is beyond the distinction of the faculties (intelligence, memory, will) or rather their return to unity.

AN EXIT THAT IS...

> The soul aspires to flee the Son just because he is the Son, in order to go all the way to the Father. It wants the Father so much, that is why the apostle Phillip said: "Lord, show us the Father and that will be enough." It wants him because he is the marrow from which flows forth the bounty. It wants him because he is the core from which spreads the bounty. It wants him because he is the root, a vein in which the bounty flows, and there, only there is the Father (JAH, Sermon 26, "Mulier, venit hora," p. 220–221).

The opening all the way to the deity is operated by the Son since, to Phillip's question, Christ answered: "How can you say: 'Show us the Father'? Do you not believe that I am in the Father and the Father is in me?" (Jn 14:9–10).

In fact, what Eckhart is aiming at is the deity, that is, the divine essence, beyond all determination and connections. We can say nothing about it, if we don't mention pure unity. For the man from Thuringia the notion of deity, at times, aims at

the Father, and, at times, grasps the idea of unity, the One
with no relationship and no method. At times, it could be the
hidden face of God; if so, we can say nothing about it.

How can we reach pure humility?

If God's essence is to give, if he couldn't but give of himself, he must then seek and find a taker, a receptive subject.
Without humility, God can give me nothing. Humility is the
condition for the diffusion of God. There will, therefore, be a
joy in being nothing in order to ask for everything. Humility
has this mysterious power to make God descend into us.

It is God's grandeur to be inclined towards what is down
below, the closest to nothingness. Also, by humbling ourselves,
we attract God. It is the co-incidence of opposites. "Those
who humble themselves will be exalted" (Lk 14:11).

It is the humble person who realizes this opening. Whoever wants to be that, that is, the greatest, God, everything,
may he become what he is, the smallest, nothing.

What is divine is that the greatest will be enveloped by the
smallest. The Incarnation aimed for that, but also for the presence of God in the soul. The highest flows into the lowest. To
Eckhart, humility is divine for it is the emergence of the sublime of God at the lowest of things (= incarnation). Through
humility (= incarnation), God is himself, outside of himself,
he makes his whatever is not his (= man), his being is exalted
(= an exit from himself). What is great for God is to be incarnated, join with the finite, the quasi-nothingness that we are
in order to take us into his arms, make us his, lift us up to
himself, all the way to the depth of what he is. Through humility, for God and man, there is an exit from the self.

The Holy Spirit is the motor of movement that leads us, a
movement that is, for us, an exit from superficiality, an entrance into the kingdom that is our depth.

...AN ENTRANCE

But this exit is, in fact, an entrance, for it operates the opening that is even more noble.

This opening is realized at two steps:

- The soul finds its prototype in the generation of the Word;
- Then the soul goes beyond this prototype; carried by the very movement of the divine Persons, it "exceeds" the trinitarian life in order to be absorbed into the unity, in a timeless instant.

The ultimate end of Eckhart's spirituality is, then, not Christ-like—yet Christ is the means since, in exteriority, we must pass by the revelator of interiority—but in the unity with God, not only in the Trinity, but in the unity itself.

For Eckhart, the One remains the highest imaginable figure of God because he is the one who expresses the Absolute with the maximum of simplicity and lack of distinction.

In the thinking of the Master of Cologne, there is a perpetual ebb and flow from the Trinity to the unity and vice versa, and the soul is not only a receptacle of this divine life, but its union to God is such that it participates in it (see Saint John of the Cross, Spiritual Canticles, paragraph 38).

The soul, which has made itself open, returns to God through the only Son. It unites to his eternal example (= prototype). It does not unite to God as creatures define him, not even to the trinitarian relationships, which are the object of the soul's spiritual attention, but to the Deity (= unity). It wants to penetrate into the "silent desert," into that "fathomless abyss," into that "source and origin." What it wants is to unite itself to the One.

In the pure deity [= unity], there is absolutely no activity; the soul only reaches perfect bliss by throwing itself into the desert of the deity, there, where there is no longer any operation or form, in order to plunge into and lose itself in this desert (AM, Sermon "Expedit vobis," p. 242).

To remain in the interior desert in order to receive this manna, to cultivate this desert in order to have this manna, that is the life of prayer. Pure prayer, in the highest sense of the word, signifies a kind of purity, not only of all bad or distracting thoughts, but of all discursive thoughts.

The essence of prayer is to frequently seek, through prayer, this intimate contact with God, where the almost total silence (it is never perfect) of the faculties could make one perceive things within oneself, to enter into the depths of one's self, to allow oneself to flow all the way to the most intimate depth of our being where God dwells and where his life shines in us.

To live for God, of God and in God, that is the secret of prayer, for to be God in God through participation, that is the duty of man, according to Eckhart.

The spirit must make its opening, God makes him within himself, and in the same way that he makes his opening in me, I make mine in him. God leads this spirit into the desert and in unity with himself, there, where he is the pure One and flowing from himself. This spirit has no reason and if it did, the unity would have to have its own reason. This spirit is located in unity and freedom (JAH, Sermon 29, "Convescens praecepit," p. 237).

We should carefully note that Eckhart's conditions for this opening are not only humility, but also nakedness of the spirit. The soul will be virginal, that is, void, purely receptive, for the image brings a determination and therefore limitations, from a condition expressed in the last word of the above citation: freedom.

Is this gift of God reserved just for a select few?

In him:

No one is so frustrated or blocked that they can't reach it, as long as, by the grace of God, they unite their will, purely and totally with God's will. They only have to express their desire: Lord, show me your dearest will and give me the strength to fulfill it…. That is why I say to you: don't be alarmed, this joy is not far from you, if you want to wisely seek it (JAH, Sermon 66, "Euge, serve bone," p. 44).

Then, the mission of the Holy Spirit is to lead the soul to the One. However, it does not work alone. It will be assisted in this exit which is an entrance, in this progression towards an identity of fulfillment.

But, remember, there can be no resurrection without a Calvary.

It is already enough to progress with the heights and the low points towards this inaccessible light where God dwells, of which Saint Paul speaks (see 1 Tim 6:16), which is pure unity.

REFLECTION QUESTIONS

In what ways do I humble myself before God so that he will find an open space to enter into me? Do I place others ahead of me in my daily life, seeking to serve those that society deems are beneath me? Do I forego something that I want so that someone in need may have it? Would fasting help me to understand what it means to be humble, to be small, to be in need of God's grace? How often do I pray that God may humble me in my life and that I will encounter him in this humility?

DAY FOURTEEN

Let God Reign in the Soul

FOCUS POINT

There is very little to actually say about God. Words do him no justice, yet we have a tendency to go on and on about God. God is an experience we must live and be present to. We have a desire to express what we feel and what we think we know about God, but we must be ready to ask ourselves at what point does this conceptualizing and attempting to understand the Divine with words become hurtful to our relationship with God. When we are too tied to the words that represent God, God cannot reign in our souls because we have become too attached to the words we use to represent the Divine.

Be quiet and don't be a chatterbox about God, for, by chattering about him, you are lying and commit a sin. So then if you

want to be without sin and perfect, don't chatter about God.
In the same way, you must not want to understand anything
about God either, for God is beyond all comprehension. A
master said: If I had a God that I could understand, I would
never keep him as God...you must totally escape from your
me-self and melt totally into his Him-self (JAH, Sermon 83,
"Renovamini...spiritu," p. 152).

W hat must be done, then, is not to chatter about God,
but to adore him: God present within us. We must, in
no way, grasp God outside of ourselves, nor presuppose anything outside of ourselves. To the contrary, we must consider
him to be our own property, like a reality which belongs to us.
It is a serious drawback to believe that God is far from us.

The soul must discover that the kingdom is inside of it.

God is in this place and I did not even know it!

Poem I
At the beginning
beyond all senses
the Word was there.
Oh how rich the Treasure
where the beginning
gives birth to the beginning!
Oh, the heart of the Father
from where, with great joy
without rest, flows the Word!
And in this womb
within himself, he keeps the Word.
It is true (Poem, Arfuyen Editions, Paris, 1988, p. 5).

Poem II
From the two, a river
of love, the fire
from two, the connection
to two together
flows the Very-sweet Spirit
in a very equal measure,
inseparable.
The Three are One.
What? Do you know him? No.
Only he knows who he is (Ibid, p. 7).

PURE CALM

All speech between the soul and God is an unjust measurement, as the soul will seek to love him: "For you, the silence is praise," and it will let God exist in silence within it.

It will draw its joy from what God is, no matter what he is.

In pure calm, the soul will be satisfied with what it is within itself: Trinity-Unity.

Eternity is now.

Past and future events, as well as those of today, are all gathered in the depth of the soul, in the present instant: the birth of God in the soul.

No one, except the soul in which God dwells, knows
what God is in a soul that loves God (MSH, Sermon,
"Et quaerebat videre Jesum," p. 87).

It is necessary to dwell in his love, that is life!

Let God be God in you. The smallest creature image

that forms in you is as great as God. Why? It takes from you a complete God (= the shrunken image), for at the moment when this image enters you, God must remove himself with all of his divinity. But God enters the place from where this image leaves...(once again, the exit that is an entrance).

My dear man, what would be wrong with allowing God to be God in you? Leave yourself completely because of your love of God. God will also leave himself completely because of his love for you (PP, Sermon, "About the Son," p. 83).

Also:

You must love him for he is pure unity, smooth and clear, a stranger to all dualities. It is into this unity that we must eternally throw ourselves (JAH, Sermon 83, "Renovamini...spiritu," p. 154).

For:

We seek your face and the face of God is his being (JAH, Sermon 59, "Daniel...sprichet," p. 196).

REFLECTION QUESTIONS

At what points in my life has God not reigned in my soul? What were the attachments that prevented God's reign? What did I rate above God and allow to reign in my life at those times? How did I overcome those false gods and drop those attachments? How can drawing on those experiences help me when I am faced with future temptations?

DAY FIFTEEN

The Awakening

FOCUS POINT

Meister Eckhart tells us: "God is more ready to give than man is to receive." Everything begins with God's grace—even our awakening to realize that an Other (God) dwells inside each one of us, that we are not alone. We must dwell at our center in the silence and solitude to awaken to Christ's Ascension within us, to the discovery that we are a part of his Mystical Body. Deeper unity between God and ourselves begins with this awakening.

One with the One, one of the One, one in the One, and one in him eternally (HN, p. 153).

TOWARDS UNITY

The epicenter of man is God. His central core is God. God comes to life in man. The Ultimate unites with him and shares his happiness. It is a co-awakening. God awakens to himself in man and man awakens to himself in God, for Christ's self becomes man's ultimate self.

Another has appeared in the most profound depth of each person's self. Each person was at home within himself, but an Other manifests himself, no longer on the exterior, but at the interior, infinitely more present in this home than the self who, up until then, believed to dwell there alone.

From now on, another fills this home up where the Other makes himself known in an instant like it is his home, like the only true home. Up until now, each person's self was the norm for all reality, the last standard. But the intimate surged in the secret part of each interiority. The self in its own dwelling finds itself also in the dwelling of the Other!

There is no beyond, for he manifests himself like the ultimate. The "me" of each is, by this very fact, relegated to the category of relative things, then the infinite makes his dwelling in the heart of each person.

The Ascension of Christ occurs in the believer.

He ascends to the most profound parts of the heart towards the peripheral zones of his being, to the horizon of the believing conscience.

From this perspective, the believer never goes to God, but it is God who awakens in man. It no longer takes a desire for God or a thirst for the absolute, but just allows God to awaken in the depth of the soul.

It takes a "dwelling at the center" where God dwells, to bore into the within in order to reach the depth of the soul appearing to be hollow and open, which opens us out onto the depth of God. It takes allowing God to be within us, since he is the center of the soul; it was Jesus who taught us to interiorize God.

Prayer in this perspective is like basking in the sun, exposed as we are to this interior light. It doesn't consist of asking this or that, or "recharging" our batteries to act or do, but to be, that is, to "commune" from within the self with the Self (God), up until the time when the self will remove himself to a level of consciousness that is more profound.

In this perspective, there are no "dwellings," no "face-to-face meetings," only a progression in awakening (see Eph 5:14), in centeredness.

> I must become him and he must become me. I will say it again: God must become, for all intents and purposes, me, and I, him, so totally one that the distinction "he/I" exists no longer and may it eternally fulfill a unique task (JAH, Sermon 83, "Renovamini...spiritu," p. 153).

Saint Paul wrote to the Corinthians: "But anyone united to the Lord becomes one spirit with him" (1 Cor 6:17). We will never finish becoming one with the One.

Once we become one, we will continue to become one. We dwell in the act of passing (to go to the Father). "Where are you staying?" (Jn 1:38), asked the disciples. And Christ replied: "Come and see" (Jn 1:39) (which means with the Father).

> May God help us become one (JAH, Sermon 16b, "Quasi vas auri solidum," p. 152).

One with the One, that is the unity of our being, of our life united as closely as possible to the divine unity.

One of the One. That would surely take a second birth. As if it was natural, the Son of God was born of the Father through grace; the Christian is spiritually born through baptism: "You must be reborn."

One with the One. Our unity could only be realized in that of God. A member of the Mystical Body, the Christian is one in the unity of this Body.

Once established in the One, we will be there for all eternity. Having been modeled after our prototype, going beyond the trinitarian relationship, we will make an opening all the way to the deity and, there, we will always advance further in the desert wilderness, which is the One.

THE JOY OF BOTH GOD AND THE SOUL
It takes one "dwelling" for the spirit at the deepest part of the self.

One doesn't need to work on forms, figures, concepts, or images, but to maintain a smooth lake in the spirit so that the "I" of Exodus will flow forth in such a way that the spirit becomes just like a burning bush. God is seethingly ontological, he is life (Trinity) in the unlimited flow of his second fecundity.

It is no longer a dialogue (conversation with God so that we feel loved), or fortuitous circumstances which suddenly produce a flash ("God exists, I met him"), but a dwelling in him, a return to what is essential, to the center where God dwells.

It takes a detachment from one's actions since their source is elsewhere, higher, deeper.

It is not necessary to practice quietism, but to make the effort to be aware that...it is an act of begging, not an act of concentration, but of receptivity. We are, then, very different from Zen or yoga. These methods aim at the human effort, but here we must wait for *everything* from God, from his grace. In this virginal intellect for all thought, in this desert wilderness, a new "sighting" of the divine arises.

It takes an awareness of the presence of God at the depth of the soul in order to actualize the union.

The other—the human brother—is no longer another. He is a member of Christ's Body on the path of realization, that is, in whom God awakens.

The joy of God emerges from the "non-science" of man's conscience.

The Christian is not a soldier, but an awakener, who seeks to make the spark of interiority burst forth.

He is a witness because it is in the great Awakening that we pass from being.

Don't seek Christ in Bethlehem or at Golgotha, but seek him in his Father, and his Father is at the depth of me. Christmas was the prototype for the birth of God in the soul.

We must let God get his joy in our souls.

The joy of God, the joy of the soul, is the participation in God's joy.

God rejoices in himself.

God's joy is in being what he is.

The soul, by participating in the unity, has truly been risen from the dead (JAH, Sermon 55, "Maria Magdalena," p. 170).

ECKHART: A WORD FROM THE ABYSS

Lord, I give you thanks for all that Eckhart has made me see, particularly the edification of man, where the justification is the beginning.

To be edified is the greatest adventure that has ever been proposed to man, the greatest risk he will ever know.

That God succeeded in elevating a creature up to him, or to speak like Eckhart, from nothingness, all the way up to him—the Being—that is proof of his love. That is what Christ brings to each one of us.

Christ told his Father: "I made your name known to them, and I will make it known, so that the love with which you have loved me may be in them, and I in them" (Jn 17:26).

Let us be assured that:

As much as God is above man, God is more ready to give than man is to receive (JAH, Sermon 62, "Got hät die armen gemachet," p. 23).

Eckhart is very demanding, for it is difficult to say:

Lord, give me only what you want to, and do what you will and how you choose (IS, p. 42).

But it is in order to realize what Saint Paul wrote (in Gal 2:20): "it is no longer I who live, but it is Christ who lives in me," that all of Eckhart's works become a magnificent commentary.

Or perhaps, it is better expressed in Jesus' words to his Father: "That they may all be one. As you, Father, are in me and I am in you, may they also be in us…I in them and you in me, that they may become completely one…" (Jn 17:21, 23).

REFLECTION QUESTIONS

Am I open to God's transforming grace in my life so that I might be awakened to his reality dwelling inside of me? As a member of Jesus Christ's Mystical Body, how does the Ascension of Christ within me move me to act in my daily life? Do I see people who I once avoided with new eyes? Do I see them as being in pain, needing someone (like me) to be present to them so that they might experience healing and renewal and unity with God through one of God's people?

Bibliography

Campbell, Karen J., ed. *German Mystical Writings: Hildegard of Bingen, Meister Eckhart, Jacob Boehme & Others*. German Library: Vol 5, 1991.

Eckhart, Meister. *Meister Eckhart, German Sermons & Treatises*. Element, 1987.

———. *Treatises and Sermons of Meister Eckhart*. Hippocrene Books, 1983.

———. *The Best of Meister Eckhart*. Backhouse, Halcyon, ed. Crossroad, 1993.

———. *Breakthrough: Meister Eckhart's Creation Spirituality*. (Image Books) Doubleday, 1980.

———. *The Man From Whom God Nothing Hid*. Fleming, Ursula, ed. Templegate, 1990.

———. *Meister Eckhart: A Modern Translation*. Harper-Collins, 1957.

———. *Selected Writings*. Davies, Oliver, ed. Viking Penguin, 1995.

Hollywood, Amy. *The Soul As Virgin Wife, Vol. 1.: Mechtilde of Madgeburg, Marguerite Porete & Meister Eckhart*. University of Notre Dame Press, 1996.

Pfeiffer, Franz. *Meister Eckhart* (two volumes). Gordon Press, 1977.

Van de Weyer, Robert, ed. *Eckhart in a Nutshell*. Trafalgar, 1998.